Automotive Web Sites

Contents

Preface

In mid–1999, the Internet boasted some 50 million users and held approximately two billion web pages making up over 190 million web sites. These numbers are growing at an explosive rate every year. If even one out of 10,000 of these sites relates to automobiles, that gives us 19,000 sites with 200,000 pages of content! Nobody has time to sift through any meaningful portion of those sites. If a person were to visit one of those automotive sites every day, it would take over 52 years to see them all, and that is assuming no more automotive web sites were ever created.

This book attempts to fill the need for a practical guide to the automotive resources that exist on the net. It is not a comprehensive catalog, but rather a directory to the most useful, informative and entertaining web sites in a variety of automotive subjects — that is, those most worth one's limited online time — plus a few to avoid so as not to waste that valuable time. It presents over 400 web addresses, describing more than 240 of them in detail. You will also find an extensive list of USENET newsgroups and automobile manufacturers' web sites.

The Internet, the Automobile and How They Work Together

The Internet has a more mature history than many of its users realize. The first true Internet was formed in 1968 with ARPANET, a network that linked the University of California at Los Angeles, SRI in Stanford, the University of California at Santa Barbara and the University of Utah. The Internet thus celebrated its thirtieth anniversary in 1998.

In contrast, one of America's oldest automobile manufacturers celebrated its one-hundredth anniversary in August of 1997, in Lansing, Michigan. This was Oldsmobile, the company founded by Ransom Eli Olds. While the automobile has had time to etch its mark on the way we see and experience our world, the Internet is just getting started. Its impact is sure to be as monumental as the automobile's.

The automotive industry has taken to the Internet like no other medium in its long and colorful history. Ford and Honda were among the first takers. According to Network Solutions InterNIC Whois database, Ford secured the Ford.com domain in 1988 and Honda secured Honda.com in 1989, years before the web truly became recognized as a viable communications vehicle in 1995. Others, such as Toyota, Porsche and BMW, were a little slower to adapt to the new medium. Toyota registered its domain name in 1994, Porsche and BMW in 1996. This relationship between the Internet and automobiles is still growing rapidly as the century passes.

Scope of Coverage

This book embraces a range of automotive subjects and gives detailed reviews and descriptions of the biggest, best, most comprehensive and interesting sites on the net. It also lists other resources such as personal home pages, chat rooms, newsgroups and more. The goal is to provide a carefully selected cross-section of the huge automotive Internet.

The number of sites is rivaled only by their wonderful diversity. You will find sites run by collectors of license plates, sites where you can buy a brand new car online, sites that cover motorsports of all types, and sites that cater specifically to women. You will also discover a great variety of newsgroups from around the world devoted to every topic you can imagine, ranging from how to swap engines in antique trucks to what kind of tires to put on your car.

There are also a number of subjects that you will not find in these pages. This is not a book about transportation sites in general, although some of the sites included, especially in the Alternative Fuels chapter, have information about mass transit and other transportation issues. You will not find sites that cater exclusively to motorcycles, ATVs, aircraft, trains, buses, bicycles, recreation vehicles, boats and other modes of transportation. These topics are beyond the scope of this book, and each could easily fill a book of its own.

Sites that were presented as interactive advertisements for a single product have been excluded. Sites that offered no informational content or were "administratively down" at the time I tried to access them have not been included, as well as sites that at one time did exist but no longer are "live" and show no signs of returning. Sites that included offensive or inappropriate content or links to such material are also omitted. More than one good automotive related site didn't make the cut because it either offered some form of mild pornography or linked to sites that did. While these sites had automotive content that would have earned them a place in the book, they had to be left by the information superwayside, so to speak.

The web sites that are presented in this book have been selected and reviewed based on a number of criteria. When it comes right down to it, content is king on the net. Sites were chosen first on the basis of their content and then other elements such as navigability, presentation and overall appeal and value based on who I thought would visit such a site. A new car buying site will be of little use to somebody looking to buy a classic car, so each site had to be reviewed with its specific audience in mind.

Change on the Internet

Change is part of the very nature of the web. Sites are constantly being created, moved and discontinued. You may find that some of the links in this book have moved or no longer exist. This is especially true for personal sites and sites that have a long non-dedicated address. For example, sites with their own addresses tend to be fairly stable and long-lasting, and usually can be found at the same address for their entire lifespan. Other sites, especially those with addresses like "http://www.serviceprovider/users/~billspage," are prone to move on occasion or simply disappear. Whatever its flaws, the web never gets stale.

Technical Notes

For review in this book, all sites were viewed on a Macintosh PowerPC computer with Netscape Communicator 4.01 or Microsoft Internet Explorer 4.0 with a 33.6 modem connection to a local Internet access service provider and 15-inch monitor set on thousands of colors.

Introduction: Searching the Web for Automotive Information

I like surfing the web just as much as the next person — perhaps a little more, since it takes up a good chunk of my free time. What I don't like is the frustration of being unable to find something I want. That is when the World Wide Web turns into a seriously frustrating experience, even for the seasoned web veteran.

For the Internet to have any value at all, you have to be able to find what you're looking for. At first, this seems like it should be exceedingly simple as there are hundreds of search engines and directories that are just itching to get your eyeballs on their ads. But not all search engines are created equal. Finding that one particular web site that can answer your question on the Internet can still be something of a challenge.

There are six primary ways to find web sites on the net. They are, in descending order of probable success:

1. **Typing in the Universal Resource Locator (http://www.website.com) or address.** This technique, of course, takes you directly to the site. It is the fastest way to get to a web site. The only problem with this approach is that you have to know the URL in advance.

2. **Specialized search engines and directories.** Every imaginable subject has at least a token directory or search engine dedicated to it. The automotive industry has six or seven very large and effective search engines — some specialized, such as Roadsters, and some general, such as AutoGuide.Net. These specialized search engines and directories offer a wealth of automotive links and are a very good place to start if you don't know the URL for the site you want to visit. Some of these sites offer additional services such as articles, message boards, newsletters and more.

3. **Directories.** General directories, like Yahoo! or Nerd World, offer huge quantities of information and links. Usually, you have to drill down through a series of ever narrowing topics until you get to the bottom, where with luck you will find what you are looking for. Many of these directories also have a search feature that will check their catalogs for keywords or even concepts. This search method usually isn't as successful as digging into the directory "by hand."

4. **General search engines.** Search engines, while popular and very extensive, are notoriously hit and miss when it comes to finding what you want. It takes time to weed out the irrelevant web sites and identify the good ones. Most search engines offer what they term "advanced search" functions, which present detailed choices and explain all of the different booleans and symbols you can use to make your searches more successful. If at first the general search does not succeed, try an advanced search.

   As well as these search features, engines are always trying to expand their services. In this effort to draw visitors, and therefore advertisers, they have created numerous "channels." These channels offer specific content and there is usually an automotive channel available. Some of these auto channels are nothing more than a very small collection of paid links, while others offer reviews, miniature directories, focused search features and more.

5. **Personal pages.** Personal pages often contain links to related subjects. If you are looking for a very specific topic, first find a general page about that topic and look for links on that page to more detailed or extensive resources. This is a good technique if you are casually looking or surfing for web sites and don't mind coming up with a number of dead ends.

6. **Guessing.** When all else fails, guess. Let's say you are looking for accessories for your new Dodge Neon. You could try http://www.caraccessories.com or http://www.dodgeneon.com or even http://www.neonstuff.com. Who knows, you might get lucky. You might be surprised what web sites lie behind random URLs. There are a number of web sites that actually are counting on misdirection to drive visitors to their content.

1
AFTERMARKET

The automotive aftermarket industry is one of the world's largest manufacturing and retail segments. This immense industry has taken to the Internet en masse, largely because the Internet offers aftermarket related businesses a low cost way to distribute their information, services and goods. It also enables the shopper to cross-reference a number of different suppliers and even to compare products from different companies from around the globe with security, ease and convenience.

E-commerce, as retail on the web has been called, has taken the Internet by storm over the past few years and consumers can now order almost anything for a vehicle of any type online via secure and safe connections. This segment of the automotive Internet is destined to only grow in the coming years, to the benefit of both the business and the consumer.

The sites that follow cover some of the aftermarket associations, retailers, general information sites and industry hub-sites, which are large all-inclusive information resources.

1

Autoaccessory.com

http://www.autoaccessory.com

Autoaccessory.com is an excellent example of the growing number of sites that offer aftermarket accessories for sale online. Autoaccessory.com offers a huge range of accessories for all years, makes and models of cars, trucks and sport utilities. Products range from running boards and tonneau covers to car covers and much more.

Visitors can also take advantage of monthly car and truck specials plus information on export sales. The web offers a unique opportunity to easily serve a worldwide market. There is also information on Autoaccessory.com's affiliate program.

2

AutoDigest Home Page

http://www.autodigest.com

This site is dedicated to anyone who works on cars, either personally or professionally. Like most other web sites, it is divided into a number of specific sections. The first, Autolookup, allows you to perform product searches on the web site. This service also includes a large number of programs which you can use directly from the site. Some of the programs include auto parts applications such as filtration and spark plug look-up; the AutoVINdicator, which allows you to determine the exact engine that is in your automobile if it was made after 1981; the Auto Manuals Lookup, which allows you to find and then purchase, if you wish, auto manuals for your vehicle; and AutoJob, which allows you to estimate the cost and time of certain repairs. Finally, there is a filter and spark plug interchange reference guide. Some of these applications also cover agricultural equipment, RVs, motorcycles, snowmobiles and watercraft as well as general power equipment. The manual lookup also includes four languages.

The site has a large auto directory that includes over 1,000 links and also features information about the auto industry, aftermarket, autobody, powersports and RVs. There are sections on automotive associations, exotic cars, export companies, vintage cars and more.

Looking for a particular chain retailer in your area? AutoDigest has a directory of them all and then some. This service also applies to Canada as well as the United States.

The site's Autoview section includes a number of "how-to" articles written by Glen Konorowski and Jody Ness. At the time of my visit there were over 30 articles available. A planned addition is Autotip, which will provide tips and tricks on maintenance and repair.

This site is a great resource for those who like to work on their own automobile, or even for those who do it for a living. It is sponsored by RepairWare, Inc., a Canadian company that specialized in automotive information technology for the aftermarket industry.

3
Automotive Aftermarket On-Line (AAOL)

http://www.aaol.com

The AAOL is an information resource for aftermarket concerns on the net. The site is broken up into several sections, and there are a few "clickable" areas, making it a bit difficult to understand where to start. Once you get the hang of the design, it's a pretty easy site to navigate.

The AAOL web site includes a number of articles and features, occasional automobile reviews, a "what's new" section, NHTSA Recall information and a link or two to automotive resources around the net. The AAOL also maintains a database of aftermarket manufacturers, associations, retailers, product links, publications and warehouse distributors. Readers can get the scoop on new aftermarket products. These new product reviews include contact information and links to the appropriate web site if available.

Visitors can find out about upcoming trade shows, get stock quotes and follow some of their handpicked links for a listing of places where you can buy or sell parts on the web.

Also offered is a "program distribution groups" directory. These groups offer support services such as purchasing, signage, marketing and advertising. The directory lists web site (if applicable), postal address and phone number.

There is also a "conference center" where visitors can participate in chat, discussion forums and other interactive opportunities.

4
Automotive Aftermarket World

http://www.aftermarketworld.com

Aftermarket World caters to the aftermarket professional rather than the retail customer. The site offers a directory of aftermarket suppliers and links to publications of interest to those employed in the aftermarket industry. Also offered is an extensive list of people from the aftermarket industry, a training guide, various training seminars, a calendar and information about the events listed. Most aspects of the aftermarket repair industry are covered, and seminars are divided up into automobile components, which include items such as the underbody, brakes, suspension and others. There is also a list of links and car pricing information courtesy of AutoWorld/VIS.

5

Automotive Service Association (ASA)

http://www.asashop.org

The ASA is an organization which includes 13,000 members who are owners and managers of automotive service businesses such as repair shops. The ASA was founded in May of 1951, and on its site you can read the group's complete code of ethics and access contact information. That's not all that is on this site.

Visitors are able to find the nearest ASA member shop or get information on *AutoInc. Magazine*, the official monthly magazine of the Automotive Service Association. There is also information about belonging to the ASA and a complete list of member benefits as well as the proper information and applications located right online.

The ASA News section offers regional event and convention information and schedules. The ASA has news on legislation and the objectives of the ASA are spelled out on the legislation page.

Visitors can also get automotive tips on brakes, what to do if involved in an accident, how to locate a respectable repair shop and more. There is also a "Tip of the Month" and an archive of the same as well as links and employment classified ads.

6

***Motor Age* Online**

http://www.motorage.com

This site, by Cahners Business Information, the current owners of the Chilton series of manuals and reference guides, is dedicated to the aftermarket services sector. It includes articles, a cover shot of the current issue and more.

Motor Age Online also offers ASE study guides. The demand for qualified technicians already outstrips the supply. *Motor Age* is trying to remedy this problem by offering study guides that you can purchase online for a reasonable price. Each study guide also offers tips on taking the test and serves as a reference manual for on the job after students pass the ASE certification. The ASE web site is described in detail in the Automobile Clubs & Organizations chapter of this book.

Motor Age serves both import and domestic automobile markets and focuses primarily on the repair, diagnostics and systems of automobiles.

There is a large archive of editorials from the pages of *Motor Age* magazine, all of which are available to read online. You can also check out a few industry links and subscribe to the magazine online. *Motor Age* also maintains a larger automotive aftermarket directory listing over 500 companies and other resources.

Be sure to check out the new products section and read "Schneider's World," which includes numerous editorials about various topics that relate to the industry, all by Mitch Schneider. The articles are well-written and often humorous and interesting to read.

7
Specialty Equipment Market Association (SEMA) Online
http://www.sema.org

The Specialty Equipment Market Association (SEMA) is the largest aftermarket related association in North America. On the design side, this site is a bit wide for a small monitor, but the amount of information included within it is astounding and overshadows any navigation hindrances that may be encountered.

This comprehensive location includes product and company finders, which are organized into a massive index by what product they provide, including apparel, filters, lights and more. Hundreds if not thousands of sites are represented in this directory. There is also a membership application, the benefits of membership and photo archives from SEMA sponsored events including the organization's huge annual show. Also, visitors can read about and explore market research, new product listings, a catalog section, an event schedule, news, a guestbook, scholarship opportunities, an "Ask The Expert" section, career opportunities and message boards. Some of these services may require membership or registration. There is even more information available if you are a member of SEMA.

8
Trucking Times OnLine
http://www.ttol.com

This simple directory features information on light truck accessories. It offers a searchable directory of manufacturers and tradenames. The search by tradename feature is useful for those who know the product, but not who makes it. As the Internet develops, web sites are challenged to offer ways to improve and expand their services. This search by tradename features is an example of a great innovation that helps readers find what they are looking for.

Additional Web Sites

9 The Expo
http://www.automobtivetools.com

10 TIP Tools & Equipment, Inc.
http://www.tiptools.com

11 Automotive Career Consultants Northern Ohio
http://www.auto-jobs.com

12 AfterMarket Online
http://www.aftmkt.com

13 Car Care Council
http://www.carcarecouncil.org

14 The ABS Education Alliance
http://www.abs-education.org

15 Viper Car Parts, Inc.
http://vipercarparts.com

16 Automotive Recyclers Association
http://www.autorecyc.org

17 PartsNet
http://www.partsnet.com

18 Automotive Sourcing
http://www.automotivesource.demon.co.uk

19 Advanced Automotive
http://www.advautotech.com

20 Automotive Career Consultants
http://www.automotivecareer.com

21 American Sports Car Design, Inc.
http://www.americansportscar.com

22 Dave Wilch's RPM Catalog
http://www.rpmcat.com

23 The Eastwood Company
http://www.eastwoodco.com

2
ALTERNATIVE FUELS

The quest for the alternative fuel that is efficient, powerful and cost effective has challenged automakers and enthusiasts alike for nearly as long as the automobile has been in existence. The idea of the electric vehicle is hardly a recent concept, as electrically powered vehicles appeared by 1887, or even earlier by some accounts.

This chapter will describe some of the best sites in regards to this journey for a "clean" personal and public transportation system. The sites covered include a sampling of the major manufacturer's efforts, along with conversions by private citizens. There are also sites here that offer components or advice, or are sponsored by associations that support alternative fueled vehicles in some manner. Some of the associations are regional in nature but offer valuable insight to the quest for clean transportation.

24
The Alternative-Fuel Vehicle Directory
http://www.vwc.edu/wwwpages/gnoe/avd.htm

A large simple alphabetical directory of alternative fuel related links.

25
Biodiesel Web Site
http://www.biodiesel.org

Chances are you've never heard of the fuel known as "biodiesel." There have been numerous attempts at altering the fuels we already use to make them burn cleaner and more efficiently, but most of these attempts have led to somewhat questionable success. Biodiesel is a refined form of plain old number two diesel that can be found at most gas stations and particularly truck stops. The site offers a low graphics version in addition to the regular high graphics version. The site is put up by the National Biodiesel Board (http://www.nbb.org).

The biodiesel web site offers a wealth of information about this form of fuel. It is divided into several sections giving the reader a general knowledge of the fuel and covering such topics as environmental impact and legislation that affects the fuel. There is also history and other information.

The site maintains a large bulletin board which takes the form of threaded discussions on all biodiesel-related topics. There is also a guestbook and a survey for site readers. One of the most informative sections on this site is the database search, which offers articles on reports about biodiesel. Each report is also available in a number of downloadable or printable formats, sometimes for a fee.

There is also an FAQ list and other informative sections covering fleet, mining, transit and marine applications for biodiesel.

26
CALSTART: Advanced Transportation Web Site
http://www.calstart.org

The mission of CALSTART is to "create an advanced transportation technologies industry and market." Its focus is on alternative fuel vehicles with some work on public transportation such as rail systems and buses.

The site offers a news section that includes current news, news archives, columns, an events calendar, press releases and more. The clean car catalog is a large directory of clean cars that is searchable by both fuel type and vehicle type. This section is accompanied by an industry yellow pages listing.

The "open user" forum is a bulletin board open to the public. There is a recharge/refuel directory for the states of Arizona and California, and at the time of this book's printing, the site's sponsor was seeking to expand this service to every state.

CALSTART itself also offers services to members of its organization, including fleet consulting, web/graphics services, CALSTART staff information, FAQs and more.

Another valuable resource CALSTART offers is its resource directory, which includes links, a glossary, technical papers, legislation and much more. In addition to this is a small classified section.

27
Drexel University SunDragon Home Page
http://cbis.ece.drexel.edu/SunDragon/SunDragon.html

Solar car racing is quickly becoming a serious pursuit of many major American universities, with over 100 viable teams competing in races each year.

Drexel University's SunDragon Solar Car Racing Team, founded in 1989, is one of the forerunners of solar racing. This site details the team's accomplishments, its cars and its team members. Sections include places where you can find information about the history of the team, photographs of the SunDragon cars, information about the team and positions available, and specifications of three of the SunDragon cars. Also included are race schedules, sponsorship information, other teams, members' bios, a guestbook, contact information and links.

28
EDS Student Engineering Activities
http://www.sunrayce.com

This site offers a great deal of information on the various races sponsored by Electronic Data Systems Corp. As sponsor, EDS provides timing and scoring, web services and engineering design analysis.

There are several races that EDS is involved with, all based on the theme of solar energy. They include the solar car race, which is the namesake of this site, Sunrayce; the solar boat race, Solar Splash; the solar bike race, BikeRayce USA; a Formula SAE race; and a Junior Solar Sprint, which is a scale model solar car race. The site provides detailed information on each of the races, including how your students and school (from elementary through college) can participate. For example, the Sunrayce section includes dates and deadlines, contact information, history, aerodynamic analysis information, press information, career opportunities, links, rules and more. The information is complete and well presented.

29
The Electric Auto Association
http://www.eaaev.org

This site, which had not been updated for four months at the time of my visit, still had useful information. Usually, a site that has been left untouched for that amount of time is considered "abandoned" and left to its own fate or has been put on the back burner in favor of other projects. Possibly neither applies to this particular site, but the site still feels neglected.

The site features chapter locations through North America, a list of the board members, newsletter information, membership information, merchandise, an electric vehicle FAQ, calendar of events, an EV (electric vehicle) business directory and a web site directory arranged by category and alphabetically. There is also a photo album of electric vehicles.

30
Electric Vehicle Association of the Americas (EVAA)
http://www.dnai.com/ev

The EVAA's mission is to promote the "commercialization" of electric vehicles in North and Latin America. This searchable site details members of the EVAA, the board of directors and the benefits of membership. Along with this basic organization information, the site contains such EV info as news, FAQs, what EV vehicles are currently available on the market and more. It also features industry news, resources, links, a directory of EV charging locations, fleet information and interviews with people in the EV industry.

31
ElectricCars.com
http://www.electriccars.com

ElectricCars.com is one of the extremely few automotive sites that use subscription memberships to access their contents. You go through several long intro screens before you must pay to go further, and there is currently no content available to non-subscribers. The site is copyrighted to a site named BikiniGirls.com.

The site promises over 50 electric car photos, specifications and reviews, plus links to manufacturers around the globe. It also claims to provide information on conventions and meetings worldwide, Internet movie clips featuring vehicles, and finally news. The site is divided into two major sections, the U.S. and the rest of the world. I cannot verify or provide information on the content of the web site.

32
Electrifying Times Magazine
http://www.teleport.com/~etimes

Electrifying Times magazine's web site is a companion site to the print publication of the same title. *Electrifying Times* magazine covers both electric and hybrid vehicles and has a great deal of racing and industry related news. On the site there is a table of contents for the current issue and a number of articles and features, with land speed records, stories and photographs of conversion projects.

33
Electro Automotive: Electric Car Conversions
http://www.electroauto.com

Electro Automotive is a company that carries conversion components for sale to do-it-yourselfers and professional converters. They offer their components both individually and in kit form. All kits are described in detail. This site also features cars for sale, a good question and answer section, books and videos, classes and workshops, and products for sale by the company, including kits by Electro Automotive. There is a price list for the products and a printable order form.

There are also a couple of services generally not seen on other EV sites. One is a large state-by-state list of trained EV component installers around the United States. Another unique free service is Electro Automotive's offer to review your proposed project and evaluate it based on the results you want to achieve in the end.

Other sections include design services, tax breaks and incentives offered by various government and private institutions. There are also links to related subjects.

34
EV Information Network
http://www.radix.net/~futurev

Electric vehicles are generally overlooked because of the public's lack of knowledge about them. Those who stop by this site and spend about twenty minutes reading will probably look at EVs in a new light.

The site features information strictly about electric vehicles and offers a wealth of information about these vehicles. Electric vehicles are subject to a number of misconceptions and the "EV facts & myths" section will dispel these myths and inform people of the facts behind EV solutions. It lists the advantages of EVs and sheds light on range and performance, two subjects that are often seen as major drawbacks. There is also a detailed history of the EV complete with a vintage photo of a very early electric vehicle and an evaluation of how the EV stands in today's ultra-mobile society.

The cost of an EV has dropped considerably over the past 10 years with the growing acceptance and availability of conversion components. The EV Information Network offers information about the realistic price of new, used and conversion EVs and their operating and maintenance costs when compared to a normal ICE (internal combustion engine). Closely related to this section is the EV conversion area, which describes in great detail the process of converting an ICE vehicle into an EV from conception to final testing of the converted vehicle. Subsections include choosing the right car, the cost of components, tools and supplies, safety, installation of key components, wiring and finally, testing.

The site's EV showroom depicts vehicles from both U.S. and international manufacturers and offers links to used electric vehicles for sale. The EV resources section offers books, magazines, newsletters, discussion lists, links, an industry directory and more. There is also a news and events section covering the EV industry.

The major component in the making of an electric vehicle is the battery, and there are a number of different types available that range considerably in price and quality. The EV Information Network has an entire section devoted solely to batteries, different types of batteries, the future of batteries and technological developments in this area.

35

EV World

http://www.evworld.com

EV World is an e-magazine dedicated to all aspects of electric vehicles in particular and alternative fuel vehicles in general. It offers an OEM (original equipment manufacturer) EV Guide to vehicles currently available from automotive manufacturers. At the time this book went to press, it offered four reviews: Ford (pickup), Honda (minivan), GM (car) and Bombardier (minicar). The Bombardier falls more into the category of "club car" or other small non-highway use vehicle. Also featured on the site are EV test drives, conversion info and an EVents calendar.

Plan on investing in the EV future? There is EV stock info on publicly traded companies that have a stake in AFV (alternative fuel vehicles) projects or components. You can also find information on EV legislation in the United States as well as interviews with people in the industry, some of which are even available as audio files. As is to be expected, the primary driving force behind AFVs, the environment, is covered. Topics in this area cover such issues as chemical pollution and climate change.

This site includes plenty of other related articles and features plus numerous audio clips of various EV related items. This site also covers some information that would be of value to racers and hobbyists of all experience levels.

36

Ford Motor Company Electric Vehicles Web Site

http://www.ford.com/electricvehicle

Ford has created a great site for learning about the basics of electric vehicles and the potential benefits they can give currently and in the future. One of the things that I especially like about the Ford site is that it assumes you know nothing about electric vehicles, and while it is commercially driven, it doesn't hit you over the head with that fact. This makes the site good for somebody who hasn't had a great deal of exposure to EVs.

Ford's simple yet well presented site offers a look into the company's electric vehicle program. It offers the potential EV buyer basic information about what an electric vehicle is, what it is not, and the basic components that make up such vehicles. A related page discusses what conductive charging is and how it relates to electric vehicles made by Ford. It is explained in everyday language that anybody can understand and offers a great primer on electric vehicles.

Another page offers information about the USABC, or United States Advanced Battery Consortium, an organization formed by the Big Three automakers (General Motors, DaimlerChrysler, Ford) in the United States to promote, study and advance the cause of electric vehicles.

There is also simple but interesting market research that provides basic information about who would potentially own electric vehicles and why they would do so. The information is not very in-depth, but offers a glimmer of the study that has gone on. Similar to this are electric vehicle charts that indicate the pros and cons of electric trucks vs. cars and give additional statistics.

Other information on this site is about Ford's "glider" program, through which qualified buyers (i.e., licensed EV builders) can purchase specific Ford vehicles without engine, transmission, ignition or fuel delivery systems. In the same vein, there is also information about the electric vehicles prepared at the factory such as the Ranger pickup and the Ecostar, a small delivery vehicle.

Overall, this is an excellent place to get basic information about electric vehicles and should be a first stop for those considering that option.

37
GM's EV1 Cars
http://www.gmev.com

GM's site is dedicated to the EV1 automobile, the first commercially available electric vehicle from one of the Big Three. If you need to know something about this vehicle, this is the place to go, and the information is targeted mainly to potential buyers. This slick and thoroughly professional no-nonsense site is divided into numerous sections. *News:* Read up on press releases, news and events and browse through the news archive. *Power:* A general information on the EV1 and a video clip of a race between the EV1 and a Mazda Miata. *Innovations:* This section details the innovations used on the EV1 and is subdivided into components such as suspension, aerodynamics, structure and more. *Features:* Safety, comfort, style and colors. *Charging:* How the EV1 recharges its electrical supply. *Gallery:* QTVR and Quicktime movies and clips. *Environment:* How the EV1 can benefit the environment. *People:* Owner biographies — who owns the cars, with testimonials. *Retailer Locator:* The EV1 is currently available only for lease through Saturn dealers in certain areas of California and Arizona. This section locates a Saturn/EV1 dealer in those areas. *Communicate:* Contact information, brochure request and links.

The site also features prices and specifications of the car and an FAQ.

38
National Station Car Association's Web Information Pages
http://www.stncar.com

The first question one might ask upon seeing the title of this web site is "What the heck is a station car?" It is an idea that hasn't caught on in the United States but has been accepted more in other countries. A station car is a form of "private" public transportation. The idea calls for a number of small alternatively fueled automobiles that commuters can rent from a single "station." Other ideas of the station car are similar to driverless taxicabs. You jump into an unoccupied station car, insert your money and drive to your destination where you either leave the car "on hold" with meter running or else just abandon it until the next person who needs it comes along and takes it. It's really an interesting way to deal with inner city transportation dilemmas. Most people don't like to take the bus, rail or subway because they have to mingle with strangers and follow the mass-transit schedule. Not so with a station car. It allows you the freedom of your own automobile while curbing congestion in inner city areas and helping the environment.

These pages offer information on a project currently under way in the

United States. The cars pictured look like kiddie-cars thanks to their shapes and primary-color paint schemes, but they are a viable means of transportation.

The site also contains information about the association itself, the concept of the station car, and demonstration sites such as New Jersey, San Francisco, Atlanta and Las Vegas. It includes an interesting photo gallery, and almost every page speaks of the benefits of electric station cars over internal combustion engines.

39
NGV.ORG (Natural Gas Vehicle)

http://www.ngv.org

Natural gas has attained a certain amount of acceptance in the motor vehicle community as a clean burning alternative fuel when compared to such technologies as hydrogen and even electric.

NGV.ORG's site includes a huge products section that lists a wide range of vehicles available with natural gas fuel alternatives — everything from refuse trucks to sedans and mass-transit buses. This section includes links to more information, engine information, transmission information and phone numbers and contact names to get in touch with manufacturers. Click on one of the links and it takes you to a page with extended and detailed information about the vehicle you have chosen.

Other sections include a page where you can locate the nearest CNG (compressed natural gas) refueling station near you. You might be surprised at how many places there are doing this. There is also a listing of events and links that related to natural gas vehicles.

Another informative section is aptly named "NGV Information," which details the benefits of NGV vehicles, including economic and environmental advantages. There are overviews of the two major types of natural gas used in vehicles, which are compressed natural gas (CNG) and liquid natural gas (LNG). There are also overviews of various engines that can burn natural gas as fuel.

The last major section is the co-funding category. This section is for those who want to convert a number of vehicles, usually for fleet applications, to natural gas. There are a number of sources that will help you finance these type of projects. Both contact information and links are provided here.

40

Partnership for a New Generation of Vehicles (PNGV)

http://www.ta.doc.gov/pngv

The PNGV is a partnership between seven federal agencies, twenty federal laboratories, DaimlerChrysler, Ford and General Motors. The ultimate goal of the PNGV is the construction of "supercar" prototypes by the year 2004. The specifications of what the "supercar" must accomplish are described on the web site. There is also a partial list of links to the partners involved in the program, what needs to be done in order to achieve their goals, program plans, accomplishments thus far and how you or your business can participate in the program. In addition to all of this, the PNGV also maintains a directory of patent information that relates to the PNGV goals and technical areas. This could be a good resource for those doing research of a technical nature.

41

Sacramento Electric Vehicle Association (SEVA)

http://www.calweb.com/~tonyc/sevahome.html

This site is mainly about what SEVA is and what it does. The site's greatest asset for nonmembers is an excellent compilation of links. There is also the usual membership information and an online newsletter archive that contains numerous back issues of the *EVUpdate* newsletter.

There is a meeting schedule and an EV Driving Test. The EV Driving Test is rather interesting as visitors can answer the "questionnaire" and see if an electric vehicle might be appropriate for them.

42

Southern Coalition for Advanced Transportation, Inc. (SCAT)

http://www.advtrans.org

SCAT's main focus is to educate young people about the advantages of electric vehicles of all types. Sections in this web site include EV Education, which points to educational resource material and events such as the EV International Challenge held at Walt Disney World in 1997, which challenged students from around the world to participate in design competitions, videotape essays and more. The site also features "hot news," consisting of articles, press releases, interviews, studies, event listings and more.

All-in-all, SCAT's web site will be of more interest to teachers than to students. The site itself does not "teach" a great deal about EV solutions, but it is an excellent repository of resources that do. SCAT is based in Atlanta, Georgia.

43
Wilde EVolutions
http://www.wilde-evolutions.com

Wilde EVolutions is an EV component supplier, but its web site offers a great deal more than just parts for sale. There are a number of photographs of EV conversions, including everything from a Series Land Rover to "Viper-eating" street cars. The company specializes in EV components, so there is the obligatory catalog section showcasing available parts. You can download a PDF (portable document file) version of the catalog for free, or if you prefer, you can order a print copy of the catalog.

The news section offers automotive history, EV history, articles on what is happening in the industry, speed record data and items such as the "Top 10 reasons to own an EV." The resource section includes an EV conversion checklist, links to other EV–related places, a discussion forum and another photo gallery. There is a classified section for those wanting to buy or sell EV parts and cars. One of the interesting things is that the site lists *other* EV parts suppliers as well, not something usually seen with online retailers.

Additional Web Sites

44 Office of Transportation Technologies
http://www.ott.doe.gov/oaat/links.html

45 World Solar Challenge
http://www.wsc.org.au

46 Winston Solar Challenge
http://www.winstonsolar.org

47 Alternative Fuels Data Center at the Department of Energy
http://www.afdc.doe.gov

48 The BombardierNV Home Page
http://www.bombardiernv.com

49 Edison EV
http://www.edisonev.com

50 American Methanol Institute
http://www.methanol.org

51 NECA: National Electric Car Association
http://www.race-neca.com

52 American Hydrogen Association
http://www.clean-air.org

53 Uncle Mark's Alternative Fueling Station
http://home.earthlink.net/~mrgasser

54 American Coalition for Ethanol
http://www.ethanol.org

55 Hybrid Vehicle Propulsion Program
http://www.hev.doe.gov

56 Honda EV+ Electric Car
http://www.hondaev.org

57 It's Electric!
http://www.greenkeys.com

58 Southern California Edison Electric Transportation
http://www.edisoncars.com

3
AUTOMOBILE BUYING RESOURCES

The Internet is quickly becoming viewed as a necessity rather than a luxury or a novelty. With the increasing acceptance of the Internet as an everyday tool, consumers have found themselves empowered with an easily accessible source for comparisons and opinions on every automobile rolling off the assembly line at any plant in the world.

This has given automobile buyers a huge advantage, enabling them to know all of their options before *they decide to purchase. Potential buyers can visit dozens of information sources and purchasing services, rather than visiting a couple of local dealer locations.*

This chapter covers a number of purchasing and information sites that offer new and used automobiles and related ownership services. One thing that is quickly evident after visiting these sites is that they all seem to offer the exact same services. Even so, the range of services available on the net is impressive. They include such items as automobile purchasing, extended warranties, roadside assistance, financing, payment calculators, links, automobile reviews, prices, free quotes and more.

59
Auto Online
http://www.auto-online.com

Auto Online, by Lease, Inc., is one of those projects that seemingly got left along the information superwayside. In other words this site, for all intents and purposes, seems to have been abandoned. There is a search function "for demonstration purposes" that would let you search for automobiles, if it actually worked. There are numerous sections, such as those that cover the company, hot news, lease returns, new car shopping, testimonials and more. The only hitch is that all of them return a "404 — File Not Found" message.

The site's design is a bit rough, as well. The opening graphic is attractive, if a bit monumental, but the design uses a frame based layout that wastes about a third of the browser's window. There is nothing in these frames besides design elements.

Perhaps sometime in the future, this site will again see the light of day, but for the present it is useless. I am surprised that the site is even allowed to stay "live" in its current state of completion.

60
AutoAccess
http://www.autoaccess.com

AutoAccess has carved itself a niche by serving only the Virginia, Maryland and Washington, D.C., area. This organization offers new and used cars, restorations, classics and other services and info.

There is a great "American Graffiti" image on the home page that will appeal to the nostalgia buffs and hot rodders. Thumbs up to a unique look for a new car buying site!

The site is divided up into four main sections. In reviewing the site, I encountered a glitch: Netscape Navigator wanted to save the file to my hard drive when I clicked on the image map that makes up the links. This was probably only a temporary problem.

61
AutoBuyer
http://www.autobuyer.com

AutoBuyer, not related to the regional magazine of the same name, is another site where you can purchase vehicles online, or at least request a quote. AutoBuyer is divided up into six main sections, the Vehicle Purchase Request section, About AutoBuyer, AutoBuyer FAQ, Information Sources, Why Use AutoBuyer and Contact AutoBuyer. Only two of these are actual content areas, but I appreciate the time the site designers took to provide the reader with some background on AutoBuyer, as this is a bit of information that many readers value but many web sites leave out.

The first section, Vehicle Purchase Request, is where you request a quote from a dealer. One thing to keep in mind, as the site states, is that AutoBuyer is not a pricing or information service, but strictly a buying service for those who are serious about buying their next car. So, in that light, this section is basically a form that you fill out and send to AutoBuyer, which will then contact a dealer. This is all with no obligation to the would-be buyer.

The information resources page is simply a small list of links to manufacturers and other automotive sites. The other sections are all about AutoBuyer and are very useful, providing the kind of information that some of the other buying services leave out.

62
AutobyInternet

http://www.autobyinternet.com

AutobyInternet is a car purchasing service that also features other support services and includes over 40,000 used cars to browse.

AutobyInternet's loan calculator is probably the best of such services offered because it takes into account sales tax, licensing and more. You can also use a related program to see a large spread of monthly payments based on what you tell it you can afford.

On the used car side are used car prices, reviews of 1994–1997 automobiles and reliability ratings. You can search through all of the listings.

The financing section includes free quotes, instant credit history checks, a 2.9 percent VISA card you can apply for online, Lending Tree (which makes lenders "bid" for your business), leasing help and the ability to compare rates within your city.

While it may not offer all the perks and services that other online car buying services have, I like AutobyInternet because of its simplicity and ease-of-use. The section covering "tips" really works more like a site directory. The navigation structure is small and tucked away but always present and available.

63
Autobytel.com

http://www.autobytel.com

One of the oldest and most well-known of the car purchasing sites, Autobytel.com does not offer a great deal of automotive information, and is essentially an automobile purchasing service. In order to streamline the process, Autobytel.com assumes visitors know what they want and intend on getting the best price available on the Internet. Visitors can search through a fairly large list of used cars based on location.

This web site offers services that allow visitors to purchase, lease, finance, warranty and insure their automobile, all from one web site. The automobile information is regulated mainly to price, photos and some reviews. Their financing section offers one-hour approval time.

Each of the Autobytel.com used vehicles has a picture, price, location and a free "lemon check." Each vehicle has also undergone a 135-point inspection and includes a 72-hour money back guarantee, plus a minimum 3 month/3,000 mile warranty.

64
AutoConnect
http://www.autoconnect.net

Search for over 600,000 used cars for sale. AutoConnect is a high profile used car marketplace with an extensive list of automobiles and a number of other features as well.

You can calculate your monthly payment, sell your car online for free, and get prices, options and other information on used and new cars. You can also compare automobiles side-by-side and have access to other reviews and information.

Although AutoConnect only lists used cars for sale, it does offer information on new cars. You can also find a dealer for a specific make in your area, get finance and insurance information, or visit the message boards. A unique free service that AutoConnect provides is called "My Notebook." With this notebook, you can keep reviews, store information such as calculator figures and even jot down your own notes. This helps prospective buyers compare automobiles in a more efficient fashion than scribbling on the back of a business card next to their computer.

AutoConnect has a nice design that makes this large site easy to use and accessible. There are advertising banners, but they have been designed into the site, and not pasted on as in so many other sites. Another nice thing is that the whole time I was visiting this site, all of the ads were for automobiles, which helps maintain the consistency of the site and really keys into the viewer's wants as opposed to catering solely to the advertiser.

65
Automobile Leasing: The Art of the Deal
http://www.leaseguide.com

Automobile Leasing is a large site dedicated to informing the consumer about automobile leasing. The topics covered include the basics—"Intro to Leasing" and "What is Leasing?"—and then expand into sections on the benefits of leasing and "who should lease." There is also a section on different types of leases. The sections are brief but informative, getting right to the point with little fluff. Anyone who is even thinking about leasing should visit this site at least once to gather information.

The navigation is easy, with a "previous topic, next topic, home" design. You can click through the pages like a slide show or go home and pick and choose.

Another great thing about this site is that it covers the nuts and bolts of how leasing works, how monthly payments are calculated, what to expect in sales tax and fees, plus the inside scoop on leasing contracts. You also get information on preparing the deal, finding good deals, negotiating and closing the deal. Other sections include a "guest experts" column and the Lease Kit, which is a complete kit for making your next leasing experience pleasant with payment tables, deal evaluation tools, worksheets, calculators and more. The only hitch is that the Lease Kit is commercial software, so you have to purchase it, which is understandable since its sales help keep this site operating. In fact the whole site is like an infomercial, albeit a very good one, for the Consumer's Lease Kit.

66
AutoSite
http://www.autosite.com

AutoSite is an automotive information resource for those who plan on buying a new or used automobile in the near future. The main focus of AutoSite is the dealer pricing reports, which can be requested through the site.

AutoSite is divided up into three primary sections, not including the "All About AutoSite" section. Area number one is the New Car & Truck Reports section, which includes fact sheets for the current model year, side by side comparisons, loan/lease calculators, rebates, incentives and more. The second section includes the Used Car & Truck Reports and has book values, recall information and the ability to search AutoSite's classified ad section. The third section covers ownership. Here visitors can get repair and maintenance information, reference sources, links, insurance quotes, finance information and extended warranties.

So, what are these AutoSite Reports all about? These reports include a detailed "at-a-glance" summary with dealer invoice prices, shipping charges, MSRP (manufacturer suggested retail price) and more. Also listed on the report will be standard equipment, optional equipment, technical specifications and engine/transmission combinations available. These reports also include photographs, color and trim, warranty information, performance information and more.

67
AutoSmartcat
http://www.autosmartcat.com

AutoSmartcat is essentially an affiliate links site, but with one major departure from the usual. AutoSmartcat locates its links with useful information in an article-like format, explaining "how to buy a car" starting with research, financing, warranties, accessories and so forth. AutoSmartcat is divided into two "paths," new and used cars. For the purposes of this review we will go down the new car path.

The first part of this process is research. This section gives information on negotiating tips, information resources on the web, how much the dealer pays and other basic facts. Then we move farther into the page, and discover that the rest is pretty much short complimentary reviews of various buying services scattered around the net. Interestingly, this site offers some editorial commentary on the *disadvantages* of buying from an online service.

The real gem in the crown of this site is its *Auto-Insider* e-newsletter, which is an interesting read and has quite a bit of information. AutoSmartcat also has its own affiliate program, a magazine subscription service and more. There is also information on finance, warranties and accessories.

Overall, this is a nice site that does put a lot of information at your fingertips and gives you an introduction into the world of buying your car online. It's obvious that this is an affiliate links site with a goal of making at least a bit of money from the links it provides, but at least there is original content as well. Again, subscribe to the *Auto-Insider*; it's worth the read.

68
AutoVantage by NetMarket
http://www.autovantage.com

AutoVantage is another new and used car buying/information megasite, but this one pitches paid membership that will get you a better deal on their services. Membership gives you benefits like coupons for free fuel, savings on car care at over 23,000 locations, car rental discounts, savings at hotels nationwide, a new car buying and leasing service and a used car buying service.

The new cars section includes new car pricing, reviews, specifications, dealer pricing, a virtual showroom with 360-degree views on select models, instant quotes on loans and leases and the ability to compare auto insurance plans.

The used car section includes car pricing, retail value and trade-in value. You can browse a used car database, post an ad to sell your car and more. There are also used car summaries including reviews and dealer pricing. Some of the services available on this site, such as financing and insurance, are provided by affiliates, which is a very common practice.

The rest of the services, such as car care, travel savings, trip routing and others are for members only, or members get special discounts or benefits. This membership plan is a unique approach, but the benefits have to be significant in order to justify it, since the competition offers some of the same services for no charge. If you travel a lot, this might be a good service for you. Remember, you don't have to be a member of this site in order to use and benefit from its primary services, new and used car buying and leasing, but you might get a preferred deal or quicker service.

69
AutoWeb.com
http://www.autoweb.com

AutoWeb.com is a new and used automobile purchasing service which also offers other related services. Visitors can sell their own car, for example, or get Kelley Blue Book prices. Some of these services have a fee; others don't.

The site includes financing and insurance information as well as the opportunity to apply for financing online, get insurance quotes, use the loan calculator to see if you can really afford that next vehicle, and get instant credit reports.

There is also an auto store where you can get such things as an extended warranty. AutoWeb.com offers roadside assistance, a bookstore and special deals on auto accessories.

Visitors are also able to research vehicles before they purchase. There is a new car showroom, recall and service bulletin information, car reviews and more. Canadian visitors can also check out AutoWeb.com Canada. There is also an affiliate program that other sites can join, and other services and information.

70
AutoWorld
http://www.autoworld.com

AutoWorld is a site that provides pricing information for new and used cars and offers free quotes on automobiles from dealers in your area. It offers several other services and informative sections as well. There are tips that cover the basics, such as invoice pricing, dealer holdback, financing, trading in your own car, service contracts and more.

Included on this site are a calculator and information about AutoWorld's parent company, VIS (Vehicle Information Systems).

One of the more unusual services that AutoWorld has to offer is a large press release section, which includes press-releases on new automobiles from manufacturers around the world.

The site also includes FAQs and automotive news. Most popular new and used cars are listed, and there is a "Cool Car of the Month." There is a glossary of automotive terminology as well as other features such as a classified ads section. The classified section includes a featured car of the week complete with photograph. An added feature available to classified advertisers is the ability to post a picture, audio or even a movie of the vehicle.

On the down side, AutoWorld has a sometimes chaotic look. Each page is a bit different and full navigation isn't available from all pages, meaning you sometimes have to backtrack to get to a whole new section.

71
Buy Car
http://www.buy-car.net

This is the mother of all affiliate banner sites. It contains nothing but affiliate banners, but it's an interesting concept nonetheless. Many of the major auto buying sites have affiliate programs, which work more or less as follows: When you post a banner on your site and somebody clicks on it and then buys a service, you get a small royalty (usually from 50 cents to a couple of bucks, depending on what the person buys).

This site has posted a couple dozen banners from various automotive affiliate programs. I found it a great one-stop source for affiliate program banners but other than that, there is no real content. The creative thinking behind the site is admirable, though.

72
Calling All Cars
http://www.cacars.com

Calling All Cars specializes in luxury, sports, exotic, classic, motor cycles and RVs, all of which are for sale by private owners. There are thousands of special interest vehicles for sale here, many of which have at least a thumbnail photo or a file photograph.

Calling All Cars also has other services that will help you sell your car, including a marketing services and a personal agent. The marketing service allows potential buyers to get detailed descriptions of your vehicle via telephone, fax or mail, and Calling All Cars has a mailing list of potential buyers to whom your car listing will be sent. The Calling All Cars Personal Agent service is for buyers. If a car that matches your criteria is added to the vehicle database, CAC will notify you with detailed information. This is a great service for those who want a specific automobile but can't spend the countless hours it may take to browse all the listings.

73
CarBuyer Internet Classified Ads
http://www.carbuyer.com

CarBuyer allows visitors to search for cars, SUVs, trucks, vans, motorcycles, RVs, watercraft, parts and more. Visitors can also place a "wanted" or "for sale" ad.

A quote service helps you get a quote from a dealer near you, and factory recall information is listed so you can check for recalls on your specific vehicle or one you might like to purchase. There is an "e-mail notifier" which works when a specific vehicle is added to the database, and the site features car chat, which is really a message board with quite a number of miscellaneous unorganized (but threaded) discussions. This forum seems kind of like a free-for-all because it contains advertisements as well as other messages. The site also has a complete "instructions" page for those having trouble with the site. There are also several links out of the site for lemon checks, warranty and insurance quotes and more. The service is also capable of supplying car dealers with an Internet presence.

This site is very simple to use and features a nice navigation structure that can be used with your images turned off. The site has been in operation since 1997.

74
CarMarket
http://www.carmarket.com

CarMarket is a used car classified site that offers information and links in addition to its primary mission of providing classified ads. The site is very simple to use and friendly to almost all browsers. You can place an ad, search the classified ads and change or delete your ad.

A "Dollars and Sense" section offers links to various sources of insurance quotes, vehicle pricing report sites, financing sites and more. There is an "Adventure" section that offers links to travel and camping related sites and a "Feature Articles" section which includes a few links and some articles about buying a car online and the future of the market. "Research Your Car" includes links to automotive review sites, as well as used vehicle history sites and used vehicle purchasing tips.

75
CarWizard
http://www.carwizard.com

CarWizard is a slick looking site that offers new and used car data, plus leasing info, free car quotes, free insurance quotes, credit reports, discounted warranties and unique CarWizard Software.

The CarWizard Software Kit includes numerous tools for buying or leasing an automobile. Unfortunately, it's only for Windows machines, so Macintosh users are left out in the cold. This software, however, allows the user to "figure lease, loans, lease vs. buy, cash back vs. low APR, early termination costs and solve for hidden costs."

It also "prints professional-looking reports for loans and leases with recommendations on improving your deal! Use the national dealer network to receive bids by fax in your own home or office!" Of course, anybody with a piece of paper, a pencil and a calculator can do the first part with a bit of time, but the ability to get bids in your own home is the truly interesting facet of this software.

The other services are the usual off-the-shelf offerings such as new and used car information and reviews. For insurance and similar services CarWizard seems to offer a few more choices than the others, however. It has three insurance affiliates, rather than one primary one, for example.

76
Classic Car Connections
http://www.classiccar-ads.co.uk

Classic Car Connections is a U.K. site that offers classic car classified ads mainly for automobiles located in the U.K. The site gives visitors the information to list their car for sale (for a fee). Visitors can also search the cars that are for sale. There is information on sponsoring the site. A car club and events listing for the U.K., editorial articles about the collector car market, a vintage racing quiz and information, and a price guide for a great number of classic cars are all included. All prices are in pounds sterling. A guestbook and a selection of music dubbed the "8 Track" complete the site.

Most of the classics for sale include a photograph, and there are a good number of cars for sale from all auto makers.

77
Edmund's Automobile Buyer's Guide
http://www.edmunds.com

Edmund's has long been a name within the publishing industry for its printed pricing guide for new and used automobiles, first published in 1966. The company's guides are some of the most trusted around. The same holds true for this excellent web site, which presents detailed information on new and used cars and trucks. It features such items as road tests, reviews, and "Buyer's Advice" on pricing, buying and financing. A "Town Hall" section acts as a discussion board divided up into numerous topics, including pickups, vans, sedans, "Smart Shopper," news and views and more. It is also possible to get rebate and incentive information through this site.

Edmund's also maintains a large section about the company itself, including a company profile, partners, FAQs, news reports, and testimonials and success stories. Edmund's Consumer Advice section includes the "Edmund's Car Buying Tutorial," consisting of 10 steps that every car buyer should follow, plus leasing information and advice. There are links to other buying/ownership sites such as financing and insurance.

There are also editorials, articles and other items from the staff of Edmund's. These include road tests, reports on innovations in the industry, humor pieces and more, and are usually worth the read.

78
Kelley Blue Book
http://www.kbb.com

KBB, as it is known on the net, is mainly about value — specifically, the value of new and used automobiles. This site offers used car, new car and motorcycle pricing. Coverage of motorcycles is one edge that KBB has over its rivals in the saturated car information market. You can find the Blue Book values of any of the above vehicle types plus dirt bikes, ATVs, scooters, mopeds, personal watercraft, snowmobiles and even sidecars.

KBB also offers listings of used cars for sale, classified so you can post your own used car for sale, as well as finance and insurance information. There are also reviews and a "Hot 50 Cars" section which includes the vehicles on which price reports were most requested month by month. At the time of my visit the Honda Accord sat on top, followed by the then new full-size Chevrolet/GMC pickups and Ford's undying F Series trucks. Half of the top ten were pickups or SUVs. Visitors can also get general information about KBB, buy the little blue book that started it all, contact the company, and read the FAQ compilation.

79
Microsoft Carpoint
http://www.carpoint.msn.com

When you have millions to sink into the creation and operation of a web site, chances are it's going to be good. In the well-established tradition of lavishly funded web sites, Microsoft Carpoint is very good.

Carpoint began purely as a vehicle information center but has grown into a full-service automobile buying and ownership site. CarPoint is all part of the huge Microsoft Network (MSN) of sites.

Carpoint offers its readers new car buying services via a free quote. The site has extensive reviews of every automobile currently available in the United States. These reviews are broken up into several sections, including cost of ownership, safety, options, technical data, overview, and usually two or three reviews by professional automotive writers. You can also check out the competing vehicles in a particular market segment.

Also featured are the used car marketplace, finance and insurance deals, window shopping, Kelley Blue Book values, recall information, maintenance information, reliability ratings, news and advice. One other relatively unusual feature on Carpoint is the availability of 360 degree surround videos of select models.

Numerous articles on the state of the automotive market are divided up into different market segments. There is a great deal of information on each of the major market segments in the U.S., including passenger, luxury, sports, SUVs, vans, and pickups.

The Auto Store offers accessories such as radios and CD changers, books and others. Visitors can use the interactive "Power Search" function to find the perfect vehicle for their needs. You may not be able to get complete information if the vehicle has just come onto the market or has just officially become the "previous" model year.

The design of this site can be a hindrance if you have a smallish monitor or a slow connection. In some sections, a large functionless top banner takes up almost half of the screen, and CarPoint employs a slow method of updating the screen. You click on a choice and instead of telling it to "go," it does so automatically, forcing you to wait until it reloads the information you have selected. This can be a bother at times, especially if you know exactly what you are looking for or accidently make the wrong choice. However, all of these annoyances are offset by the sheer amount of information that the site contains.

80
N.A.D.A. Appraisal Guides
http://www.nadaguides.com

The National Automobile Dealers Association offers several things of note on its small but tidy site. Visitors are able to purchase any one of the organization's several guides online including the used car guide; the classic, collectible and special interest car guide; the motorcycle, snowmobile, and ATV and personal watercraft guide; the marine applications guide; and the recreational vehicle guide.

In addition, you can research values online, visit the links page and learn about N.A.D.A.

81
Net-A-Car
http://www.net-a-car.com

Net-A-Car specializes in special interest automobiles of all types. You won't be able to buy a spanking new car here, but you will find restored and original classics, conversions, street rods, kits, sports and performance cars, investment cars, exotic and "world class" cars, the rare and unique, unrestored antique cars, parts cars and more. There are also featured cars available for sale.

For example, if you want a "Rare & Unique" automobile to impress the neighbors and click on that section, you'll find four choices. Picking "One of a Kind," you get a list of years broken up into decades. Picking 1960–1969 yields a large list of automobiles, but the "One of a Kind" description is an overstatement. There are dozens of cars for sale, but none of them could safely be described as a true one-of-a-kind vehicle. A 1967 Ford Fairlane turns out to be a restored hot rod with blue flames, for example — somewhat unusual, but there are other flamed hot rod Fairlanes running around out there. What Net-A-Car lacks in category specificity, however, it makes up with sheer numbers and variety.

The number of cars available is staggering. If one were looking for a special interest car to purchase from a private seller, this is probably one of the first three resources to check, the other two being Trader Online (http://www.traderonline.com) and the *Hemmings Motor News* print magazine (http://www.hemmings.com).

An enormous number of interesting autos is not the only trick up Net-A-Car's sleeve. It also offers a search feature, a free car screen saver, other net resources and links, information about the site and the company and more. You can sign up for its affiliate program. The company also maintains a large number of sister sites including:

http://www.vettesforsale.com
http://www.streetrodsforsale.com
http://www.musclecarsforsale.com
http://www.classiccarsforsale.com
http://www.antiquecarsforsale.com
http://www.specialtycarsforsale.com
http://www.classicsforsale.com
http://www.antiqueandclassiccars.com
http://www.specialinterestcars.com
http://www.car-buff.com
http://www.automobilesites.com

The Net-A-Car series of sites is among the best automotive site networks on the net.

82
StoneAge
http://www.stoneage.com

StoneAge is a full service automobile buying service which features both new and used vehicles. It offers price quotes from a dealer near you on vehicles from 1993 to the current model year and offers over 200,000 used vehicles for sale from this web site. Visitors can search the used vehicles by state or search the entire listing. StoneAge offers a full service car buying service that guarantees the lowest price. This service uses an auction process which puts several dealers in competition to make the sale. StoneAge reports that this usually works best on big-ticket vehicles with lots of margin and special hard to find vehicles. This is a fee based service.

The site also offers car prices and reviews, and visitors can sell their car for a fee. StoneAge has partnerships with several other automotive sites that offer support services such as financing and insurance. Visitors who have web sites can also sign up for StoneAge's affiliate program. Finally, there are the expected testimonials and general information about the company.

83
Trader Online
http://traderonline.com

Trader Online is a huge directory of used vehicles for sale by private parties and dealers around the United States. This site is a companion to the series of *Trader* magazines. The main feature of Trader Online is the huge selection of vehicles for which you can search. All of the searches can be performed by price, model, make, location, keyword and other criteria.

Each section also has other features, such as listings of interesting sites that relate to that subject. There are postings of job opportunities at the Trader home offices, awards the site has won, a page to help you with the site, contact information, advertising information, a loan calculator and other features.

One of the amazing things about Trader Online is that there are more than just cars and trucks. There are currently ten sections on Trader Online. At the time of my visit, the site contained: Auto Trader with 614,020 vehicles, Collector Car Trader with 19,346 entries, Pickup Trader with 161,604 trucks for sale, Cycle Trader with 24,613 cycles for sale, Boat Trader with 35,459 boats, RV Trader with 14,462 RVs, Aero Trader with 884 planes for sale, Big Truck Trader with 24,574 heavy trucks, Heavy Equipment Trader with 14,544 pieces of equipment and finally Bargain Trader with over 53,000 great deals on all sorts of stuff.

84
The Web Carshopper
http://www.carshopper.com

The Web Carshopper is a turn in a different direction from most purchase-oriented car sites. Rather than a buying or quote service, it is strictly a source of automotive information for new and used car buyers. However, this site is affiliated with AutoBuyer, a site that does not offer automotive information, but is strictly a quote service.

The Web Carshopper is broken up into four main sections: "Visit the Dealers," "Gather Information," "Browse the Used Cars" and "Information About AutoBuyer/Web Carshopper."

The dealers section includes only dealers in a select number of states and provides links to those dealers' web sites, or sites constructed and hosted on Carshopper's site. You should not look to new car dealer web sites for impartial information, however — you'll find that they *all* have the lowest prices and *all* of them have the best selection and *all* of them have the friendliest staff.

There are a limited number of links, and the used car section is a huge one-page alphabetical list of used cars for sale by dealers and private individuals. The list appeared to be three to four months old at the time of my visit.

The Web Carshopper does contain some useful information, but not enough to warrant a bookmark when compared to some competing sites. The entire Internet car buying segment is saturated, and it takes a huge amount of information and services to win the consumer's click.

Additional Web Sites

85 Warranty Direct
http://www.warrantydirect.com

86 CarFax
http://www.carfax.com

87 CarFinance.com
http://www.carfinance.com

88 AutoMall USA
http://www.automallusa.com

89 AutoRow
http://www.autorow.com

90 Cars.com*
http://www.cars.com

91 Vehicle History Reports Online
http://www.vhronline.com

92 AutoNation USA
http://www.autonation.com

93 AutoPro
http://www.autopro.net

94 AutoExact
http://www.autoexact.com

95 CarSpot.com
http://www.carspot.com

96 World Wide Wheels
http://www.wwwheels.com

**Home of the* Car Talk *web site, featuring sound from the radio show, staff biographies, polls, puzzles, car reports, a database of recommended mechanics, merchandise, and a vast amount of other material.*

97 Autoguide.com
http://www.autoguide.com

98 National Auto Research Black Book
http://www.blackbook.net

99 IntelliChoice CarCenter
http://www.intellichoice.com

100 Autoplace
http://www.autoplace.com

101 Online Auto Car Buying
http://cartv.com/

102 Car-List
http://www.car-list.com

103 Carbiz.com
http://www.carbiz.com

104 The Personal Car Shopper
http://www.personalcarshopper.com

105 CarSmart
http://www.carsmart.com

106 The Land Rover Exchange
http://www.lrx.com

4
AUTOMOBILE CLUBS & ORGANIZATIONS

Chances are, if more than two of any particular automobile were ever produced, there is a club or organization that is dedicated to that automobile. Car clubs give enthusiasts an opportunity to share their passion with those of like mind. They also offer individuals the ability to acquire parts and information more readily. A large number of these clubs have a web site that features events schedules, photographs and detailed information on their vehicle of choice.

Professional organizations are another facet of the automotive industry. Many of these organizations have a presence on the Internet, and many of their web sites contain substantial information about their chosen topic.

This chapter explores both of the above groups.

107
AAA Online
http://www.aaa.com

Everyone has heard of the AAA and seen its famous Triple "A" logo-mark on the back of vehicles. This organization has existed since 1912 to assist motorists and travelers of all types and make their travel time safer, cheaper and more enjoyable.

AAA's national web site starts with a page where you enter your zip code. After you have done this, you are taken to your specific state's home page. I reviewed the Wisconsin site and describe it below, but it is safe to expect other states' listings to be similar.

This large web site offers its members and visitors tons of information about both the services offered by AAA and services offered directly from the web site itself, such as online tourbooks and direction services. The site is extremely easy to navigate and has been designed with eight main sections, most of which lead to additional content pages.

Automotive Services: AAA is known mainly for its automotive services, and this section details such services as roadside assistance and automotive tips that help you care for your automobile and travel safely. *Traffic, Maps & Routing*: Online tourbooks, detailed direction services and related items. *Financial Services:* Special rates on car loans, lease terms, credit cards, mortgages, checking and savings accounts. *Insurance:* Special services and quotes on auto and home insurance. *Travel & Reservations:* The club's many travel services such as passports, international driver's permits, reservations, weather and construction reports and much more. *AAA Savings:* Specials on entertainment tickets, tours, cellular phones and more. *News & Info:* Tips and resources for driving, safety and travel.

Of course, the site offers the obligatory membership application forms and a benefits handbook.

108
American Automobile Manufacturers Association (AAMA)
http://www.aama.com

The AAMA is the oldest automotive trade association in the United States and can trace its inception to the year 1900. This organization focuses on DaimlerChrysler, Ford Motor Company and General Motors. Its web site offers a wealth of industry data and statistical information covering these automobile manufacturers in the United States. Their site lists the usual contact information, office locations and other basic information, but once you get past all that there is a massive collection of data.

Some of the major sections of this web site include industry data such as automotive forecasts, production and sales figures, import penetration into the United States, truck sales, employment, and financing trends. The range of data available on this site is astounding. Interestingly, this organization no longer offers its publications for sale since all of their data are now posted on this web site. That makes getting all of this great information even easier.

Another facet of this site is measuring the impact that automobiles and auto makers have on the economy, society and the environment. Environmental impact is assessed on several levels including, but not limited to, car recycling, emissions, safety issues, fuel economy and what the future may bring.

109
American Automotive Heritage Foundation
http://www.classicar.com/tradeorg/aahf/aahfhome.htm

This is the site of an organization whose mission is to "preserve, protect and promote the automotive heritage of the United States through public education and related activities." The AAHF was established in 1994 by a $75,000 grant from *Hemmings Motor News* (http://www.hemmings.com). The AAHF's mission is to provide grants to organizations that protect, preserve and promote the rich and varied automotive heritage that has developed over the past 100 years. They seek to promote public awareness, and their site includes quite a bit of information about the foundation — including the names of those on the Board of Directors, who happen to belong to some other highly recognizable classic and antique automobile organizations. There are also press releases, projections for the future of the foundation and a statement of the goals of the organization. The site solicits donations and provides a printable form for your convenience.

If you feel that your organization could warrant a grant from the American Automotive Heritage Foundation, the site provides detailed information on what should be included on grant proposals and how the consideration process works.

110
American Truck Historical Society (ATHS)
http://www.aths.org

The ATHS is an organization dedicated to trucks and the history of trucking and claims a membership roster of over 20,000 members from over 20 countries. Their trucks are all at least 25 years old.

This web site holds a large photo album of many classic, antique and historic trucks ranging from trucks built in the very early 1900s to more recent editions. Another interesting thing about this club is that the trucks they support range from heavy working trucks to smaller light trucks. Anther section that will bring back many memories for old truck lovers is the stories page. Here you can read stories that feature antique trucks as their centerpoint. The stories are informative and entertaining trips down memory lane. The site includes a calendar of old truck events, a Mack truck trivia challenge, classified ads with many classic and antique trucks for sale, a special members-only page, a state by state listing of club chapters, a discussion forum and information about *Wheels of Time*, the organization's publication. Books, videos and other products are available, and the usual information about how to join the organization is provided.

111
Antique Automobile Club of America (AACA)
http://www.aaca.org

The AACA maintains a large, informative web site that is presented in a simple, eye-pleasing format. The AACA is, according to the web site, the largest and oldest antique car preservation society in the world. Its mission is to preserve, restore and maintain antique, classic and significant automobiles. Ownership is not a prerequisite to membership.

The site offers a wealth of information regarding the AACA headquarters, officers, membership, local clubs, coming events, the AACA Museum, Inc., the club's many publications, legislation, judging, and videos and films. There are links to regional and chapter clubs and finally a discussion forum. The officers section includes information on past and current officers. The legislation section includes information on national, state and local legislation; what the AACA's role is; the club's legislation policy; and tips on how to write effective letters to your representatives. The judging section includes information on the five primary classes of cars represented at AACA–judged events.

112
Association of International Automobile Manufacturers, Inc.
http://www.aiam.org

AIAM is an international association of automobile manufacturers that produce and distribute vehicles in the United States. Every major manufacturer that produces or distributes in the United States is a member of this association. The web site is designed in a unique way. Navigation is straightforward, but the site's design is very colorful and chock full of elements. This makes loading a tad slow but not as one might expect; the images must be well compressed.

The site breaks into a number of sections including notes on the globalization of the industry, production in the United States and how it stacks up with other countries, new plants that have been built or are being built in the United States (most notably by foreign auto makers), how the automotive industry impacts the U.S. economy, community involvement, money raising events, community support and other topics. A section called "The Socially Responsible Automobile" covers economy, safety, quality, technology and related subjects. Milestones of the industry, links to member sites, and driving and car care tips are also listed.

113
Audi Quattro Club USA
http://www.quattroclubusa.org

The Audi Quattro Club offers basic information about its club and the benefits of joining, which you can do online. It currently claims more than 2,500 members. There is an events schedule along with some photos and summaries of past events, links, a mailing list and an online version of the club's publication, *Quattro Quarterly*. On the down side, there is really no information here about the automobile the club is dedicated to.

114
Australian Automobile Association (Ausauto)
http://www.ausauto.com

The Australian Automobile Association maintains this small site, which consists of two content sections plus some support pages. Content section number one is the *Motor Equipment News* (*MEN*) area. *MEN* is a publication that addresses mainly aftermarket equipment for, you guessed it, motor vehicles. Listed are subscription information, back issues, a table of contents for the current issue, advertising information and a number of recent articles.

The second content area is the Trade Fair section. Ausauto promotes the annual Australian Automotive Trade Fair, and this section includes information on the convention such as registration services, floor plan, dates, times, costs, locations and so forth.

The site also features advertising information, feedback and hot links.

115
Automobile Association (AA United Kingdom)
http://www.theaa.co.uk/theaa

The AA is not unlike its American counterpart, the AAA. Its large site contains quite a few services and content areas for motorists in the U.K.

Here, visitors can join the AA; get specials on auto, home, motorbike and travel insurance; and order books, maps and CD-ROMs covering popular travel destinations. There are hotel booking services, driving school listings, postings of employment opportunities within the AA, finance and loan quotes and more. The entire site is searchable by keyword.

Also included is information on buying a used car, safety, fuel prices around Europe, crash test results, advances in automotive technology and other topics. Some of these services may be limited to members only.

116
Automotive Parts and Accessories Association (APAA)
http://www.apaa.org

The APAA web site offers a huge amount of information on the global aftermarket parts and accessories industry. This is one of the most comprehensive aftermarket sites in existence at this time.

The site includes background information on the APAA, including an aftermarket overview that details the sectors of the industry and their sales trends. There is also a list of major aftermarket events around the world, as well as information on current legislation and regulatory efforts (much of which is archived). The site also contains members-only news, job listings, links and more.

Another major section is devoted to market research. Foreign and domestic data are presented, and reports are for sale to members and non-members. The site details miscellaneous publications such as the *APAA Factbook* and *Mini-Monitor,* among others.

International trade overviews of Japan, China, Latin America and other regions are featured, along with commentary on environmental issues, health and safety, Year 2000 issues, and various other topics. Educational and training materials and programs are described, and a book list is maintained on the site.

117
Automotive Service Excellence
http://www.asecert.org

The familiar phrase "ASE certified technician" refers to the certification of mechanics by this organization. The web site includes a great deal of information about the 440,000-member organization and what it does. One section that will be of interest to prospective ASE technicians is a listing of test information on the following tests: Automobile, Medium/Heavy Truck, Collision Repair and Refinish, Engine Machinist, Alternative Fuels, School

Bus, A/C Recovery and Recycling, Parts Specialist, and Advanced Engine Performance. This should be the first stop for anyone who is considering taking any of these tests. Instructions for registration are provided.

The ASE also maintains a "Virtual Toolbox" which gives prospective technicians the "tools" they need to successfully become ASE certified. Training resources, links and career information are covered in this essential section of the site.

"Tips for Motorists" includes car care, a "Women's Corner" and a great deal of consumer information. Blue Seal Facilities — shops that have earned the ASE Blue Seal certification — are the subject of a separate section, and the site offers downloadable applications in several formats for shops that seek to have their site certified as a Blue Seal Facility.

There is also information on the National Automotive Technicians Education Foundation (NATEF), which is an organization related to the ASE that evaluates training programs.

There is also a great deal of information on Team ASE Racing. The organization fields a truck in the NASCAR Craftsman Truck Series, and a section of the site tells about the team. There are also links, a "What's New" section and other features.

118
Buick Turbo Regal Web Site

http://www.gnttype.org

This site is for owners and aficionados of all turbocharged Buick Regal models, 1978–1987, including the T-Type, Grand National, and GNX. It contains background information on the cars; model-specific maintenance tips; guidelines for performance modifications; photos, videos and sound files; listings of part numbers and sources; classified ads; an events calendar; hot links; and various other tidbits for enthusiasts.

119
CamaroZ28.com

http://www.camaroz28.com

CamaroZ28.com is a premier fourth generation F-body web site owned by Chris Frezza and Jason Debler, both of whom own high performance Camaros. Although this web site isn't a club per se, it is a gathering point on the web for thousands of Camaro and Pontiac Firebird enthusiasts. The main focus of this site is the fourth generation Chevrolet Camaros, produced in the 1993 model year and after. (Generations are generally marked by major body style and engineering changes. For example, Chevrolet's Corvette is currently in its fifth generation; hence the Corvette's C5 designation.)

CamaroZ28.com offers its readers a number of resources. It includes exclusive articles such as reviews of cars and aftermarket products. There is also a great F-body FAQ section, Java and IRC ("Internet Relay Chat") chat, streaming video, links, awards and a credits page. However great this all may be, the crowning achievement of CamaroZ28.com is its "Ultimate Bulletin Board." Here you can browse through over 15,000 posts by F-body enthusiasts on all manner of products.

120
The Car Club
http://www.thecarclub.com

The Car Club is a great idea that has never really reached fruition. The main cause of this delay is the fact that most of this site has been "coming soon" for a very long time. It has six main areas, only three of which were really operational when I visited. The best section by far is the nice looking photo gallery, divided up by marque. They include, but are not limited to, AC Cobra, Bugatti, Cadillac, Delahaye, Duesenberg, Ferrari, Jaguar, Mercury, Porsche, and Rolls-Royce. There are a number of excellent photographs of classic cars here. The site also includes a bulletin board (which is coming soon and will feature classified ads and a calendar), a marketplace, and a gift shop with a few items for sale (most of this section, too, is "coming soon"). The last two sections are also interesting, especially the "Gearheads" section, which includes games that you can play online or download. The selection is limited but what is there is well done. Also be sure to visit the Club House and read the road trip articles.

I can only hope this site will expand its offerings. What is here is really very good, but the slow arrival of most of the promised content is disappointing.

121
Car Clubs World Wide
http://www.carclubs.com

This site does basically one thing, and does it very well: It lists car clubs and events. You can list your club or event for free, or you can search the events by state or country. But this is just the tip of the car club iceberg. There are hundreds of club listings here from around the world. Almost every type of automobile (plus a couple of other modes of transportation) is represented. Each car club listed is described by the following items: contact name and position, club name, address, phone, vehicle type, dues, URL and e-mail address. Each club has a one-line blurb regarding what it is about.

122
Classic Car Club
http://www.classiccarclub.org

This is the official site of the Classic Car Club of America, a group formed in 1951 and dedicated to the preservation of 1925 to 1948 vehicles designated as classics. Most of the site's content concerns the club itself—history, publications, events, meeting reports, activities, membership and the like. There are also classified ads and photographs of several notable classics, however. See fuller entry in the Classics & Hot Rods chapter.

123
Coalition for Vehicle Choice
http://www.vehiclechoice.org

The Coalition for Vehicle Choice has a mission that seems fairly simple in a country like the United States. The group seeks to "preserve the freedom of Americans to choose motor vehicles" such as SUVs and light trucks. The site offers a great deal of information about this goal. There are articles and features about airbags, fuel economy, light trucks, SUVs, vans, new technology, major issues in Washington D.C., global climate issues, emissions, safety and consumer tips.

Another feature is the *Update* newsletter, which you can read online. You can also browse through the back issues, new releases and links.

124
DeLorean Motor Club
http://www.delorean.net

This DMC site is a simple one-page information site strictly about joining the club, and includes contact information and an online membership form. There is no information about the automobiles.

125
DeLorean Owners Association
http://www.delorean-owners.org

The DeLorean Owners Association maintains a large and very informative web site dedicated to an automobile that was produced for only a brief time during the early 1980s. This car, made famous by the *Back to the Future* movies, is the stainless steel bodied DeLorean. This easy-to-navigate site is divided up into several major sections, and each of them into smaller subsections. Navigation is achieved through the use of a simple frame layout that gives you access to the entire site.

The section titled "The Legend" is dedicated to the car in particular, detailing the history of the marque and the man behind it, John Z. DeLorean. There is a detailed description of the car including complete specifications. A picture gallery is included as well as buyer's tips and most interestingly, design differences between individual DeLorean automobiles. Certain design features changed from one run of cars to the next because of the challenges of working with stainless steel. This commentary not only shows the changes, but documents why they were implemented.

The site also details regional and national event schedules and maintains a large list of museums around the United States that have DeLoreans on display.

The publication section includes information on the group's publication, *DeLorean World,* and gives information on back issues and a technical index, giving members the opportunity to find articles in specific back issues — a service which has to be a great help to any DeLorean owner or enthusiast. There is a small "What's New" section as well as the usual membership information and a marketplace. The marketplace includes books, posters and other memorabilia.

126
Durango Owners Club
http://www.durangoclub.com

Chrysler rolled out the Dodge Durango in 1997, and the Durango Owners Club (DOC) was founded shortly thereafter. The club was incorporated as a nonprofit organization in the spring of 1998.

The club's goals are to support Durango owners and potential owners through a variety of services. The site lists the organization's constitution and bylaws, membership benefits, how to join and a list of corporate members.

The real content of the site comes with two other sections, the DOC Forum and the FAQs. The Forum is a large bulletin board where owners and potential owners can ask each other questions and make comments in a focused environment. The other section, the FAQ compilation, is truly remarkable. The FAQ page covers five major sections of information: operation, accessories, new buyers, maintenance, and performance. Dozens of questions are answered in detail.

If you own or plan on owning a Dodge Durango, this should be your first stop on the web the next time you log on.

127
Edge Racing
http://www.edgeracing.com

Edge Racing is a members-only wholesale club that offers auto related merchandise at wholesale prices. Although the site does not offer any e-commerce capability at this time, it does list the benefits of joining the club. Membership information is provided, and you can apply online. The site prominently displays a privacy statement, so submitted information should be treated confidentially. There is a form you can use to request more information about the club, and a brands page, which displays the logos of some of the major brands you will be able to purchase through the club.

Edge Racing maintains a 36,000 square foot physical location in Miami, Florida. This sort of wholesale club looks like it could become a good idea for both the business involved and the consumer. On a down note, the site is too wide to fit on a 15-inch monitor.

128
Emergency Vehicle Owners and Operators Association (EVOOA)
http://www.intrlink.net/evooa/index.htm

The EVOOA is a club that promotes and supports vehicles that were used in public service, such as police, fire, ambulances, hearse, tow trucks and others. The club was formed in May of 1996 and the site includes a membership application form.

There are several good sections on this site: the members' vehicle index, classified ads, upcoming events, past events, links and the non-member photo gallery. The members' vehicle index offers a couple of dozen links to members' web sites where they showcase their vehicles. The classified section is coming soon and the upcoming events section includes event information and contacts for events that will happen in North America. There is also some information on the EVOOA's past events.

A large section is the non-member photo gallery. There are currently 26 galleries with such headings as police cars from the 1970s, police cars from Chicago, fire trucks from particular locations and so forth.

129
Foothills Street Rod Association
http://fsra.org

A street rod club located in Calgary, Alberta, Canada. This site is the home of Rodlinks, a nice list of pre–1949 street rod links, and Autolist, a list of other autolinks.

130
Ford Galaxie Club of America
http://www.galaxieclub.com

This club's charter states that its mission is to preserve 1959–1974 Ford Galaxie passenger automobiles built by the Ford Motor Company. This site offers a table of contents to the current issue of the *Galaxie Gazette*, the club's newsletter/magazine, and there is an archive of past issues of the *Galaxie Gazette*. Included are sponsor links and technical information and statistics such as production numbers, list price when new, and prices of restored vehicles. There is a page dedicated to technical tips that will be of use to Galaxie owners. In addition, there is membership info, plans for the club's future, a photo gallery, links to some of the club's chapters across the United States, member classified ads, event coverage and listings, articles relating to Galaxie topics of all types, a state-by-state listing of auto museums and more. There are also members-only forums and articles.

131
Grim Rides Funeral Car Club
http://members.aol.com/hearseq/grimrides.htm

Got a hearse? Well, Amy the Hearse Queen, president and founder of Grim Rides, does, and so do a bunch of other people that are part of the Grim Rides Funeral Car Club located in San Francisco, California. Items of note on this web site include message boards, a gallery, a photo album, an interesting FAQ section covering funeral cars, cars for sale (hey, what are you waiting for, get your hearse today!), hearses in the movies (both automobiles and horse drawn), links and much more. Grim Rides is a good read for any automotive enthusiast because it covers one of the more unusual sections of the hobby, and it's hard not to smile when you see a photo of a Cadillac hearse with a flame job!

132
Horseless Carriage Foundation, Inc. (HCFI)
http://www.hcfi.org

The non-profit HCFI was established in 1985 "to make automobile research and restoration information readily available to hobbyists, restorers, and scholars worldwide." The HCFI maintains a library in La Mesa, California, that holds mainly pre–1916 materials but also has information on vehicles of all types through the year 1965. The foundation also holds, and seeks, archived materials and historic memorabilia.

The HCFI provides a range of valuable information services to anybody interested in the group. It will do research for you upon request for specific information. The HCFI charges a fee to offset the costs of doing the research; all prices are listed on the web site and vary by the level of research or information you are requesting. After you have made a research request, the organization will contact you with a more specific price and availability. The selection of materials is very broad and the site includes an "index of archives" that includes the following headings: Automobile Company History, Automobile Historic People, Automobile Marques (Makes), Automobile Quarterly, Coffee Table Books — Photo Books, General References, Miniature Cars, Pedal Cars, Periodicals, Advertising, Serial Number Guides, Transportation, Trophies, and Trucks. Visitors can also become a member of the HCFI, and with that membership come some special privileges in regards to getting research performed at the library.

133
International Amphicar Club
http://www.amphicar.com

There are not very many automobiles that have to be registered both as a car and a boat. Of those few, the Amphicar is usually the first to come to mind. Approximately 3,000 of these cars, built in Germany in the 1960s, came to the United States. Years later, the International Amphicar Club was formed. The web site lists a meet schedule, club members list, a brief but informative history of the car, photos of vintage ads, a list of museums, classified advertising available to both members and non-members, club merchandise, a discussion group and other features.

One of the more unusual items of this site is a chronicle, complete with photographs, of a club member's resurrection of an Amphicar that, to the unaccustomed eye, would have been written off as a total loss to be sent to the wreckers. Another nice thing about this site is that it shows the original specifications of the car and a "standard parts list," which shows commonly needed parts and part numbers and some conversion information.

134
International Hot Rod Association (IHRA)
http://www.ihra.com

Much like its counterpart the NHRA, the IHRA includes competition results, schedules, news, point standings, statistics, a track directory, a large multimedia photo gallery of drivers, membership information and contact information. The IHRA covers both professional and sportsman categories of drag racing motorsports.

135
International Motor Contest Association (IMCA)

http://www.imca.com

The IMCA covers modified, late model, sprint car, stock and hobby stock classes. IMCA events are open to "anyone ready to take on the challenge of climbing into the driver's seat." If you feel up to the challenge, you can get a detailed description of all five of the IMCA classes. Everything from the entry-level Hobby Stocks to the Modified class is covered.

Included on this site is a track locator for all seven regions in the United States, and you can also look up tracks by state. Each track includes location, type of track, type of race, promoter, phone, specific location and a link if applicable.

One of the interesting bits on this site is a listing of sponsors along with their addresses, phone numbers and what type of race they sponsor.

Visitors can also get rule updates for all five classes and news updates by month. You can order apparel only via a 1-800 number, but you can view the products, sizes and prices online. Finally, there are the IMCA Forums and classified ads.

136
Kaiser Frazer Owners Club

http://members.tripod.com/~ben1937/kfoci.htm

Information on the Kaiser, Frazer, Kaiser-Frazer, Henry J, Darrin, Allstate, and Willys Aero or Jeepster series of vehicles is the specialty of this club site. It offers a guestbook, a monthly bulletin whose current content is detailed on the site, information on a mysterious document know as "The Handbook," and information on how to contact the club historian for information about the marque and the men behind it, Joseph W. Frazer and Henry J. Kaiser. The Featured Cars section displays photographs and descriptions of a small number of cars. There are also pictures of collectibles such as advertisements and vintage postcards and information on *The Quarterly*, a quarterly magazine dedicated to K-F issues. A members page and links are also offered.

137
Maserati Club International

http://www.maseratinet.com

The Maserati Club International maintains a large site that mostly contains information about the club, although there are some valuable resources here in addition to club information.

The club information side of the site contains membership information, background on the club, club publications, a back issue index, a list of services that the club performs and a membership roster.

The Maserati Club International also has a commercial side, the MIE Corporation. This company maintains a 30,000 square foot facility and deals mainly in technical information and spare parts for Maseratis of all years. It holds a cache of spare parts worth over $12 million. Maserati Club International members enjoy discounts on parts and services from MIE.

You can place orders and get quotes online from MIE or from a printable form. Other items supplied by MIE are accessories, books, manuals, performance parts and conversion kits.

MCI also maintains a bulletin board, classified ads, a photo gallery, Maserati news, and links.

138
Mercedes-Benz Club of America
http://www.mbca.org

The Mercedes-Benz Club of America is dedicated to helping owners "preserve the appearance, performance, and value of your Mercedes-Benz, new or old." The club was established in 1956 and is now over 30,000 members strong from regions in the United States and Canada. You can click on the history button and get the whole story, as well as a list of regional directors and e-mail address, if applicable. Another sidelight is information about the MBCA's magazine, *The Star*, named after the marque's classic logo.

Members also have access to the MBCA Technical Hotline, a telephone service through which you can get quick answers to technical questions. This service is available only to club members. Also along the lines of technical support, there is the MBCA List, an e-mail mailing list that is free to club members.

Along with a calendar of smaller upcoming events divided into National, Regional and Section, the MBCA site also has information on StarFest, the MBCA National Convention, which is the primary MBCA event held annually. MBCA–hosted events are held all around North America.

You can also apply to the MBCA online via a secure form and visit links to related sites.

139
MG Car Enthusiasts' Club
http://www.mgcars.org.uk

This magnificent site is perhaps the greatest source for information on MG on the entire Internet, providing much history of the marque in general and detailed information about particular models. For each model, the site gives a detailed history, notes on styling and design, images, paint codes and specifications on chassis, steering, brakes, wheels, engine and much more. This informative resource is huge.

Also included on the site are articles on motorsports and insurance, classified ads, bulletin boards, a picture gallery and a fine listing of other resources. There is also information on *MGenthusiast* magazine.

140
Military Vehicle Preservation Association (MVPA)
http://www.mvpa.org

An international non-profit organization dedicated to the collection, preservation and restoration of military vehicles. Although there isn't a great deal of information on military vehicles on this site, the site does a good job at telling people about the club and its publications, the *Supply Line* and *Army Motors*. It offers links to related sites, a listing of events, contact information and some other information not directly related to the MVPA, but still relevant to historic military vehicles.

141
Minnesota Street Rod Association (MSRA)
http://www.msra.com

The MSRA maintains a large multisection web site on which you can take a look at numerous pictures of events from around the state, read some of the better e-mail that the site has received, sign the guestbook, take a look at members' pages, read about the year in review, learn about the group's "Adopt a Highway" program, visit links, and find information on upcoming events. You can also apply for membership, e-mail the board of directors and sponsors, and see the Street Rod of the Year plus other award winners. The cars are depicted by excellent illustrations.

Like most regional clubs, this site will be most useful to those who live in that particular state, but a general street rod enthusiast can also benefit from visiting.

142
National Corvette Restorers Society
http://www.ncrs.org

Dedicated to the restoration, preservation, history and enjoyment of Corvettes made from the model years 1953 through 1982, this very well designed site is the home of the NCRS, which was formed as a non-profit group of enthusiasts in 1974. Information on membership, *The Corvette Restorer* magazine and the bimonthly newsletter *The Driveline* is provided, as well as dates, times and locations of the club's events. The NCRS offers Corvette related merchandise as well.

143
National Hot Rod Association (NHRA)
http://www.nhraonline.com

The NHRA is one of the major sanctioning bodies of racing in the United States. Its site offers a wealth of information on NHRA races and member teams, including a schedule of events divided into national events, races in special classes and divisional events. There is a track directory with links and information on tracks that the NHRA runs on.

There are race results, ticket information, statistics such as records and point standings, directions on joining the NHRA (and a list of benefits), classified ads, rule revisions and more. Visitors can also take a look at driver profiles, TV schedules, merchandise, tutorials on drag racing and more. The NHRA covers only professional drag racing motorsports.

144
National Motorists Association
http://www.motorists.com

Founded in 1982, the National Motorists Association's mission is to be an advocate of the American motorist. This site includes the "Motorists' Bill of Rights," which is what the NMA feels every law-abiding motorist deserves. This site lists the benefits of membership and contains links and a complete section on fighting speeding tickets. The NMA Store offers books, tapes, bumper stickers, and other merchandise. The site states the association's positions on key motorist related issues such as daytime running lights, emissions, speed limits and more.

145
NRMA Limited
http://www.nrma.com.au

The NRMA is a company in Australia that offers a wealth of information and services to its members. This is a large, easy-to-use site dedicated to motorists in general, and members of NRMA specifically. Sections include membership (benefits of joining NRMA include roadside assistance, technical services, legal services and others), financial help pages, crash test reports and insurance estimate services.

About half of the information presented on the site is reserved for members only, especially in the travel section of the site. The motoring section includes vehicle operating costs, road tests, buyer's guides, automobile prices and more. There is also a "your money" section that offers a great deal of content.

146
Opel Association of North America
http://www.opel-na.com

The most well known Opel ever to make it to American shores is without doubt the Opel GT, which was often referred to as looking like a baby Corvette, although there is no relation between the cars. The OANA serves not only these vehicles but also other Opel autos found in North America. Unbeknownst to many, the Cadillac Catera is closely related to an Opel automobile not available in the United States.

The Opel Association of North America was formed for the purpose of providing a source for locating parts, service and technical help, and a forum to exchange information with other owners of all U.S. imported Opel models from the 1957 Olympia to the gray-marketed Opels of the 80s. The Opel Association has an emphasis on the Opel GT, Manta "A", Ascona "A" (aka 1900 model) and Kadett models, which were the primary Opels imported to the U.S.

Most of the club's web site services are available to anybody, though some sections are understandably limited to club members. Those sections are the Tech Tip Library, the Value Guide, the downloadable newsletter and an archive of past issues.

The OANA offers membership to a mailing list and access to the Classic Opel Email Archive. Its site contains a message board, links to Opel related sites and businesses, membership information, events, parts sources, classified ads, pictures, history and other items. The list of parts sources includes "business card" ads for suppliers of parts around North America.

147
Pantera International
http://panteracars.com

A factory authorized club for DeTomaso enthusiasts, this site offers information about the vehicles themselves, a bulletin board, a guestbook, a club store, chat, a photo gallery with excellent photos of the cars, parts and cars for sale, links, coming events, benefits of joining the club and information on the group's quarterly publication.

148
Porsche Club of America
http://www.pca.org

Official site of the Porsche Club of America. The PCA site offers extensive information on the organization, which boasts over 138 chapters located within the United States, Canada and Germany. The site provides information on *Porsche Panorama*, the club magazine, driver education, autocross programs, concours, technical data, a PCA "vocabulary" and other subjects. Also included on the site is the usual information on how to join the club.

149
Shelby American Automobile Club
http://www.saac-mcr.com

This large site is dedicated to all Shelby automobiles. There are photos of Carroll Shelby and articles about him; a classified section where you can purchase cars, parts and services; a monthly calendar of Shelby related events; and the opportunity to visit and sign the guestbook. Carroll Shelby is a big chili fan and in that light, the SAAC-MCR has a special chili page with recipes and coverage of chili cookoffs around the country.

The Cobra Showcase contains images of the infamous AC Cobra that Shelby took to astounding heights. An original Cobra can sometimes bring as much as $200,000 at auction, and the present-day AC Cobra is arguably the most popular kit car based on an actual production model. The AC Cobra is actually a car built in England with a big block Ford engine.

The site also has an online magazine called *Shelby Life* with articles about Shelby American, Carroll Shelby's company that produced the Shelby Series I and the Shelby Cobra, as well as other Shelby concerns and features of cars. Past issues are archived. Last but not least is the links section, which has great links to other Shelby sites.

150
The Tucker Automobile Page
http://www.tuckerclub.org

If there is anything that you need to know about the Tucker automobile or Preston Tucker, the man behind it, this is the very first place you should look. This site was created by the Tucker Automobile Club of America and features huge amounts of Tucker related information. Here you can join the club (a must for any Tucker enthusiast) or shop for books, stickers, model cars, caps and other merchandise at the Memorabilia Shoppe. Want to find a TACA convention near you, such as recent events held in Ypsilanti, Michigan (the birthplace of the Tucker), and Las Vegas? Then check out the calendar of events. Other features include a chat room, a bulletin board, the *Tucker Tribune* (an e-mail newsletter), and a fact sheet which includes the Tucker's "vital statistics" such as width, horsepower and more. Find out how to own a Tucker and get a surprise bit of info on the images page about Alex Tremulis, chief stylist at the Tucker Corporation between 1947 and 1949.

On the down side, you can get lost in this site easily. An inconsistent use of the design can hinder navigation, and some links take you without warning out of the site. Great info, but the layout could use refinement.

151
United States Council for Automotive Research (USCAR)
http://www.uscar.org

USCAR was formed in 1992 by the Big Three to research and consider "new opportunities." These technologies, covered in the "About Specific Technologies" section, include recycling, reuse, recovery, batteries, lightweight materials, new engine designs, alternative power sources, safety, making advancements affordable, emissions and more.

There is also detailed information about the "FutureCar" project, which challenges students to build the "FutureCar." The top engineering schools in North America are participating in the challenge. The idea is that students are given a car chosen by USCAR and the students must modify it to achieve certain goals. Complete details are on the site.

The USCAR site also maintains a huge Media Center, which provides press releases and information on the various technologies presented by the USCAR. There is also information about the related PNGV, Partnership for a New Generation of Vehicles, which was established September 29, 1993, and is similar to USCAR.

152
Vintage Mustang Owners Association
http://www.vntg-mustang.com

The VMOA is a regional Mustang club located in San Jose, California, that was founded in 1977 to "provide a focal point for Mustang owners who wished to further their enjoyment of ownership." The club includes all model years of Mustang. You do not need to be an owner to join the club; being an enthusiast is enough.

There is a schedule of VMOA meetings, information about the VMOA, information on their Adopt-a-Highway program, listings of member home pages, a vintage Mustang chat room and links. There is also a club application which can be printed.

One of the things that will interest all types of classic automobile enthusiasts is the site's coverage of legislation in California. California has a long history of being exceptionally hard on hot rods. This site covers current and past legislation that has sometimes significantly helped the hobby and in other cases hurt it.

The VMOA site is simple and easy to use with what is known as a "first generation" web site layout, meaning that it is basically a simple page with no real design flair and primarily text. This makes it kind of dry, but accessible.

153
Weekend Mechanics Club
http://www.weekendmechanicsclub.com

The Weekend Mechanics Club addresses repair and maintenance of automobiles for the average weekend or shadetree mechanic. There's no tech-talk, no run-arounds, just simple straightforward help in a highly usable design.

The site offers a parts store locator that you can use to find a parts store in your area. There are also numerous feature articles on auto repair and maintenance, covering everything from basic to more advanced automobile repairs. Everything from how often you should change your oil to "getting to know" the various filters that your automobile uses is covered.

There is a parts finder, a coupon finder, tips and links. The links are divided by category, and there are numerous quick tips on maintenance and repair. You can also join the club for free and get information on contests, promotions and more.

The Weekend Mechanics Club is sponsored by the Automotive Parts and Accessories Association.

Additional Web Sites

154 Jensen Interceptor Owners Club
http://www.jioc.org

155 Volvo Resources: BrickBoard
http://www.brickboard.com

156 A4.Org
http://www.a4.org

157 Mopar Alley Automobile Club
http://www.moparalley.org

158 Club DSM
http://www.dsm.org

159 Fiero Owners Club of America
http://www.fieroowners.com

160 Riviera Owners Association
http://www.rivowners.org

161 The AMX Files
http://www.amxfiles.com

162 Corvair Society of America
http://www.corvair.org

163 Rolls-Royce Owners Club
http://www.rroc.org

164 TruckClub.com
http://www.truckclub.com

165 Southern California Mini Truck Council
http://scmtc.ml.org

166 Mini Madness
http://www.minimadness.com

167 International Volkswagen Association
http://www.ivwa.com

168 Prowler Club of America
http://www.prowlerclub.com

5
CHAT

Chat is one of the web's early accomplishments. It allows netizens to communicate in real time at no additional cost. To this point, the ultimate form of Internet based chat comes with Internet Relay Chat (IRC). The only downside to IRC is that it requires specialized software, a good connection and some arcane knowledge of the commands needed to use the system. Meanwhile, web based chat systems offer simplicity of use in exchange for a more cumbersome and slower interface. All of the major browser based chat rooms require registration of some sort. Smaller, personal sites and IRC do not.

The software required by IRC is called an IRC Client. Popular IRC software can be obtained at any download site such as TuCows (http://www.tucows.com). After you have downloaded the software, you can visit EFnet (http://www.efnet.net) or DALnet (http://www.dal.net) to learn how to use IRC. In addition to these two popular IRC nets, there are many others that you can explore.

EFnet offers the following auto-related chat channels: cars, moparmuscle, mopar, chevy, grandprix, and hotwheels. DALnet offers one called buickgn.

169

Auto OnRamp: Automotive Chat

http://www.autoonramp.com

Auto OnRamp, now part of Talk City, is a more extensive version of Talk City's "bare bones" chat rooms. Auto OnRamp features more in the lines of content such as auto care forums divided up into manufacturer, book store, discussion groups, real chat rooms, special chat sessions with race car drivers and free home pages, based loosely on the GeoCities "neighborhood" model.

170

Car Forums — Automotive Message Forums

http://www.carforums.com

Car Forums is a relatively new service that offers numerous forums and live chat. A search engine is also included, but it was kind of slim at the time of my visit. In order to post messages, you have to register, but this process is quick and simple. The goal of Car Forums is to provide a complete question, answer and discussion forum for enthusiasts from around the world. All of the separate forums are divided by manufacturer and the site gives you the opportunity to search through all of the posts.

171

OmniChat!'s MotorChat

http://www.4-lane.com/motorchat/index.html

OmniChat! offers several different browser based chat rooms, including car, boat, motorcycle, 4x4, classic and RV. MotorChat does not require any sort of registration.

172

Talk City

http://www.talkcity.com

Talk City's chat topics included autos, classics, general, lowriders, motorcycles, new cars and racing at the time of my visit. The overall usage seems to be heavier than the WebChat Broadcasting System.

173

WBS — WebChat Broadcasting System

http://pages.wbs.net

The WBS offers a chat environment without Java, plug-ins or anything else. It is a totally browser based chat system. It can be tedious over slow connections, but if you have a good connection you shouldn't have any problem. The auto, motorcycle and racing sections don't see much action here.

6
CLASSICS & HOT RODS

Classics, customs, antiques, hot rods, street rods and other special interest automobiles have a strong showing on the web. This is so because the enthusiasts behind such automobiles are passionate about their hobby and that passion translates to the web very well. It offers even average shadetree mechanics the opportunity to showcase their pride and joy to the world.

There are also some very large and comprehensive sites that cater to the special interest automobile enthusiast. On these sites one can often find car club listings, parts resources, links, pictures and much more. This chapter covers a number of classic and special interest sites that are certain to provide enthusiasts with a great deal of valuable information.

174
Auto Restorer On-Line
http://www.autorestorer.com

Auto Restorer is a large site that is full of great restoration information. No matter what you are restoring or what stage you happen to be in, this is a great source of information. There are also tips for the repair and maintenance of restored cars.

Some of the sections on the site include a project gallery featuring projects "in the works" and links to sites on the web that show restorations in progress. There are also numerous content sections that offer beginning and advanced restorers all kinds of info. This section includes tips, a Q&A, and a number of forums divided up by year or type of automobile. Visitors can also take part in Resto Chat or browse a very large bookstore, classified ads, links, car show listings and quite a bit more.

The Articles section is one of the best and most useful on the net devoted to automotive restoration. There are numerous articles covering all sorts of restoration topics. Another thing that makes this web site visitor friendly is the "utilities" page. These utilities are items such as e-mail, a guestbook, awards, advertising information and other web site related tools.

175
AutoRoad
http://www.autoroad.com

AutoRoad is a large site dedicated to classic cars of all types. The only hitch is that the site does not fit on a 15-inch monitor, but this is a minor concern when weighed against the amount of information the site presents to its viewers.

AutoRoad, like every web site on the net, is under continuous development. Some of its features were "in progress" at the time of this writing but will probably be in full swing by the time this book is published. AutoRoad features a wide range of technical information, including tune-up, specifications, VIN, color codes, engine information and more. There is a selective collector car price guide, free classified ads, car chat, a picture gallery, historical articles, Q&A forum, show and event listings, a bookstore and a huge selection of auto supplies. The auto supplies section seemed unusual to me. AutoRoad offers over 4,000 automotive items for sale — everything from car care to restoration supplies. At the time of my visit online processing was in development.

176
Classic Car Club of America
http://www.classiccarclub.org

The CCCA is the "official" classic car club, the group that determines what cars are to be recognized as classics. Think a '57 Chevy is a classic? Well, think again. Actually, nothing after 1948 is considered a classic by the CCCA, and even cars before 1948 have to meet strict criteria to qualify as classics. One of the good things about the CCCA's web site is that it lists what the club considers classics and the criteria they use to determine such issues.

The CCCA sponsors a number of events, and you can find more information about their annual meeting and other events on the site. Another feature is the history of the CCCA, which was founded in 1951 in order to preserve "truly distinctive" automobiles. There are also a few nice photographs of notable vehicles.

This site is surprisingly limited, considering the influence this organization wields in the collector car hobby. The most valuable information is the contact data and the criteria for what constitutes a classic car.

177
Classic Car Source
http://www.classicar.com

Classic Car Source is one of the most comprehensive classic car sites on the net, especially if you are looking for links to clubs, articles and the like.

The site does suffer from frequent "broken pipe" errors. I have been visiting the site for about two years using three different ISPs and two modems, and I always get at least one or two "broken pipe" errors per page. This is usually remedied by reloading the page, but can get tedious if you have to do it repeatedly.

Classic Car Source claims to be "the world's largest online community for the classic vehicle enthusiast," and the claim is hard to doubt. The site includes featured articles on classic vehicle issues such as repair, restoration, number matching, and parts locating, and there are also stories and articles on vintage racing. The articles are archived so you can take a look at past features. The site includes reader's comments and a classic truck section (http://www.classictruckshop.com) that makes up its own web site; it also offers live chat, forums and classified ads.

One of the most comprehensive lists of club links can be found at this site as well. There are hundreds of clubs listed and hosted on this site. Chances are there are at least a couple that specialize in your particular classic vehicle. Other directories include parts, services, dealers, museums and events. The museum directory is very large. Also take a look at the book store and online communities.

178
Classic Cars
http://www.classicars.net

Classic Cars offers a large directory of links for classics both common and rare, old and new. It has links to some of the best sites on the subject. Each section offers a list of links, a form to add your own link and a photo of the vehicle covered. A partial list of their sections includes Alfa Romeo, AM General, Cobra, Austin-Healey, Marcos, Panther, Lotus, TVR, Westfield, Mustang and more.

179
Classics4sale.com
http://www.classics4sale.com

Classics4sale.com has gone from a rather obscure site selling a couple of old cars to a veritable clearinghouse for classic cars and trucks. The site is divided into 5 main sections: classic trucks for sale, classic cars for sale, wanted to buy, how to post an ad and classic auto links. There is no extra charge for a photo and minimum run time is currently three months for a price that's lower than most, if not all, monthly car seller magazines. There are also links related to classic car restoration and enthusiasts, along with some manufacturer links.

180
Dallas Mopar Web Community
http://www.musclecar.net/dallasmopar/

Mopar owners will be drawn to the Dallas Mopar Web Community by the mountains of information that webmaster Brian K. Harshaw has accumulated here with the help of fellow Mopar enthusiasts. Here you will find a guestbook, editorials, a monthly top 10 list along with archives of the list, Java Mopar chat, a discussion board, classified ads, reader's polls, a parts supplier directory, and VIN information (including '68–'71 B-body, '64–'65 Mopar, and '68–'74 general). The site also features a car of the month and production numbers on select models. The image gallery covers trucks, modern Mopars, Chargers, A, B, and E bodies and more. There are also links and information about the site and its dedicated webmaster.

181

Gilmore — Classic Car Club of America Car Museum

http://www.gilmorecarmuseum.org

The Gilmore car museum was opened to the public in 1966 and features over 120 cars housed in five historic Michigan barns. There is the typical information about admission, hours and location. There is also a page telling the history of the Gilmore Car Museum and its involvement with the Classic Car Club of America.

Among the more recent items on the site is information about the museum's new interpretive center, which will be similar to a 1930s filling station and is being built brick by brick. There is a schedule of events and car shows as well as information on features and exhibits.

182

Happy Days

http://www.hdays.com

Happy Days, while not necessarily an automotive related site, offers memorabilia from the golden age of hot rods and classic cars. Happy Days offers tin signs and memorabilia related to such subjects as Betty Boop, Coca-Cola, Elvis, Marilyn Monroe, James Dean and Route 66. You can purchase directly from the web site, and all of the items available are described and shown in a good photograph. Although the site claims that the online ordering form is secure, neither Netscape Navigator nor Microsoft Internet Explorer showed that the page was secure via their "lock" icons normally associated with a secure web page. A mailing address and phone number are also provided for ordering, however.

183

Hemmings Motor News

http://www.hemmings.com

Hemmings Motor News ("the Bible of the collector car hobby") is a large publication listing items and services for sale primarily in North America but also from around the world. *Hemmings* is the ultimate parts and car resource book for those looking for a specific item, and if it's not listed directly in *Hemmings* there is a good chance that somebody who can find it is.

Hemmings' web site is a limited form of the magazine, but has several unique features, such as the Hemmings Store, which offers model cars, planes, banks, clothing and subscriptions; information on their other publications, such as unique calendars and the magazine *Special Interest Autos*, the Hemmings Vintage Auto Almanac and unique publications such as "How to Get Started in the Old Car Hobby."

Another item of note is the listing of Scam Alerts. *Hemmings Motor News* takes complaints against its advertisers very seriously and posts information about verified scams that may affect readers of the publication. There is also a monthly listing of stolen collector cars.

184
Hot Rod Garage
http://www.hotrodgarage.com

The Hot Rod Garage offers classified ads in categories for cars, trucks and "other automotive," which seems to be a catch-all. Hot Rod Garage is also a Trader Online affiliate, so you can search Trader Online (described in the Car Buying chapter) directly from this site. The classified section also includes club items and want ads, as well. Visitors can also sign or read the Hot Rod Garage guestbook.

Visitors to this web site should also visit the photo gallery, which includes a featured car and a number of great shots of hot rods and street rods. There is a forum entitled Bench Racing and some tech tips covering all manners of hot rodding.

185
Hot Rods Europe
http://www.hotrodseurope.com

Hot Rods Europe is a large site dedicated to "the support and promotion of Street Rods, Hot Rods, Custom Cars, Classic American Cars, Kit Cars [and more]" specifically in Europe. The site consists of a number of sections including news, events, feedback, search, links, info about Hot Rods Europe, discussion, virtual club nights, video clips and more. The site also hosts some car club web sites such as the Victory Wheelers Street Rod and Custom Club, a club which supports the same ideals as Hot Rods Europe.

Some of the sections are self-explanatory, while others, like "virtual club night," are unique to this site. The Virtual Club Nights are scheduled Java chat sessions, and the discussion boards are a small collection of posts about appropriate topics.

186
HotRodder.com
http://www.hotrodder.com

HotRodder.com offers free and paid premium memberships for automobile (primarily hot rods and classics) related sites. It offers chat, a book store, a virtual car show, classified ads, new aftermarket products, a guestbook, links, "my first car" stories, featured cars and other items. HotRodder.com offers descriptions of its members' sites on a single page.

187
My Classic Car
http://www.myclassiccar.com

My Classic Car is a companion site to the TV series on TNN by the same name. The site is a large compilation of classic car sites. There are numerous articles covering the history of selected makes and models, other topics, comments and current news. There are also restoration tips, a Q&A section, classified ads, a classic car club registry, a vendor directory that is searchable by location (national, international, Internet), a bookstore, and more.

There is a Fun & Games section that includes auto trivia, a photo gallery, a scrapbook, chat and other features. There is also information on the *MCC Magazine*, an industry directory entitled the MCC Motormart, purchasing MCC merchandise online, and becoming a Certified Car Nut and joining Club MCC. There is a large list of benefits associated with membership in Club MCC detailed at the site.

188
1 in a Million Classic Cars
http://www.1inamillioncars.com

1 in a Million Classic Cars is one of the gems of the Internet. This is a good all-round classic car site offering message boards divided by decade (1920s through present), auto chat, a user survey, cars for sale, auto parts for sale, photo ads, want ads and more. There are also a small but high-quality selection of images in the reference/image gallery, links (including classic car club links), a classic car quiz and a cartoon of the day. This web site also features project cars.

189
RoverWeb
http://www.off-road.com/RoverWeb

RoverWeb is a web site that offers a huge amount of information about Land Rovers in general and the older Series Land Rovers in particular.

Most importantly, this site jointly holds the Land Rover FAQ compilation with the Ottawa Valley Land Rovers (http://www.ovlr.org/), which is the "oldest and largest Land Rover club in Canada." The FAQ covers Land Rovers from 1948 to the current model year. The FAQ section is a large collection of general information on such topics as specifications and identification of various models. An introduction covers "general information" as well as how to join the Land Rover mailing list. The actual "General Information" area covers the history of the marque, advertising, and how to decode serial numbers, build sheets, production numbers and so forth. There is also "Other Useful Information," which includes parts suppliers, clubs, publications, links and other topics. There is a section on identification and a section on vehicle specifics that covers repair and maintenance plus articles and newsletters. Finally there is the "Other Miscellaneous Information," touching on such subjects as the Camel Trophy, famous Land Rover owners and the Anti-FAQ ("silly answers for silly questions").

RoverWeb also includes Gasoline FAQ, Motor Oil FAQ, Winch FAQ, and Coolant FAQ sections, an owner mailing list, and other features. Some of the FAQ pages are links to outside sites.

190
Viper World
http://www.viperlist.com

Chrysler, the original muscle car company, revived its image as a hard hitting maker of world class sports cars in 1992 when its Dodge division rolled out the all-new V-10 Viper, the first "true" muscle car to come out of Detroit in years.

Viper World celebrates this car in all of its testosterone laden glory. The site offers a tech section for owners that includes tips and tricks for modifying and improving their cars. Visitors can also get information on Viper World's news groups and the Viper List, a mailing list maintained by Viper World for Viper enthusiast and owners. Here visitors can read the Viper List FAQs, join the list or sign off the list.

There is an accessories section that includes information on parts and accessories as well as a large and detailed directory of suppliers. Also included in this site are event listings, drag race photos, links, a gallery and a guestbook.

The site also offers downloadable PDF versions of its newsletter and maintains a classified ad section in which you can purchase or sell Viper cars and parts. There are also non–Viper related items in the classified section such as the Plymouth Prowler, the Viper's cousin over at Plymouth.

Additional Web Sites

191 Chevy Muscle
http://www.chevymuscle.com

192 Buick Bombsight
http://www.classicar.com/bombsight

193 Coker Tire
http://www.coker.com

194 426hemi.Com
http://www.426hemi.com

195 VintageAutos.Com
http://www.vintageautos.com

196 The Filling Station
http://www.fillingstation.com

197 Collector Car Restoration
http://www.carestoration.com

198 The Classic Car Place
http://www.classiccarplace.com

199 Henry Ford Museum & Greenfield Village
http://www.hfmgv.org

200 Mopar Collector's Guide
http://www.mcg-pub.com

201 Classic Industries
http://www.classicindustries.com

202 Hot Rod Nostalgia
http://www.hotrodnostalgia.com

203 Old Cars, Like New!
http://www.oldcars.com

204 BumpStop
http://www.bumpstop.com

205 Blue Moon Gear
http://www.bluemoongear.com

206 The Big Blue Car
http://www.kustoms.com

207 Car-Trek Classic Car Headquarters
http://www.car-trek.com

208 The MGB Experience
http://www.mgb.bc.ca

209 Muscle Cars For Sale
http://www.musclecarsforsale.com

210 Rusty Hope
http://www.rustyhope.com

211 MoparParts.Net
http://www.moparparts.net

212 The Street Rodder Network
http://www.streetrodder.com

213 Vintage Cars: Mining Co.
http://vintagecars.miningco.com

7
COLLECTIBLES & MOBILIA

There are numerous hobbies associated with automobiles. There are enthusiasts who collect everything from the real article to die-cast replicas and license plates and all other sorts of automobilia, as it is called. Collections of advertisements, gas station memorabilia, road maps, gas pumps, hood ornaments and mascots, literature and endless other items dot the web. Some of these sites can be great resources for both the beginner and the advanced collector. In addition to those who collect such items, those who sell them are well represented on the net. This chapter offers an overview of the types of automobilia to be found on the web.

214
Art Cars in Cyberspace
http://www.artcars.com

Art cars are a phenomenon that has existed since the beginning of the automobile. Now they have found their way into cyberspace. Art cars are vehicles that have been transformed into works of art — not panel vans with airbrushed scenes of scantily clad barbarian women riding polar bears, but the literal transformation of an automobile into a rolling piece of art. Most people have heard of cars covered with sod, or seen pictures of cars decorated with hundreds of light bulbs, made up like a Holstein cow, or covered with bottle caps. These are the true art cars.

Art Cars in Cyberspace celebrates these automotive wonders with a large collection for those merely interested in looking at artists' works and for those adventurous souls who decide to turn their vehicle into a mobile work of art. The home pages feature articles about what's happening in the art car scene and on artists and their autos. There is event information, pictures, stories, advice on how to make an art car, a gift shop and more. The entire site is searchable and detailed in a simple site map.

Their giftshop includes T-shirts, videos, books, calendars, screen savers, postcard books and many other items. Something that will be of interest to potential artists is the "Making of an Art Car" section, which covers the tips and tricks of the trade, including such information as what adhesive to use. There is also information on how to make your vehicle a "temporary" art car so you can clean it off when you're done having fun.

Another great section of this site is a directory of art cars on the web and stories and backgrounds of several dozen art cars with photographs of the vehicles themselves.

215
Auto Trend Graphics
http://www.autotrend.com

Auto Trend Graphics specializes in the sale of automotive posters. Hundreds of posters are available for purchase via secure online ordering or phone. The only problem with this site is that it is image intensive so it loads very slowly, unless you have a very fast connection. Once it does load it's great, offering some looks at interesting vintage posters.

The site includes posters from a large number of categories including Mercedes-Benz, Race Car Drivers, Formula 1, Lamborghini, Porsche, History, Motorcycles, Muscle Cars, Technical Cut-A-Ways, Classics and many more. While the primary focus is on reprints of vintage racing posters, there are posters on other subjects.

Auto Trend Graphics also offers other items, such as mousepads, custom framing, clocks and watches. You can search all of these posters and items by make of automobile.

There is a links page, as well. On the design side, other than the graphics-heavy implementation, the site can be viewed as both framed and unframed versions. This site has come a long way since its inception and has continuously added to its inventory and range of products available.

216
Autoliterature.com
http://www.autoliterature.com

Autoliterature.com offers all manner of automotive literature for sale through its strictly online catalog. It features OEM manuals, buyer's guides, and motorcycle, tractor and truck related books. They also carry the complete line of Chilton publications, the leader in aftermarket repair and maintenance manuals. There are a couple of other sections of note on this web site, as well. They include a letters section and an editorial called Conrad's Corner. There is also a good selection of links.

217
Autorama
http://www.autorama.com

Autorama has a bit of information that will be of interest to nostalgia buffs. It features information about automobiles on stamps and the stories behind them as well as a small but interesting archive of automobile advertising. There are print ads of classic and antique cars ranging back to 1888, and each is accompanied by a photo of the ad, clarification on what the ad says and even some information about the car or the company featured in the ad. There are also TV commercials available to download; including, for example, the 1950 Mercury and the 1958 Chevrolet and Edsel.

I have only minor complaints about this. I would like to see more ads and more video clips, but I understand that much of this material is hard to come by and copyrighted, so distribution over the net can be a challenge. The site uses a frame layout that utilizes only about two-thirds of the browser's window with active content. The rest contains logos and in one case a small navigation feature. But since the site only includes two or three content areas, this could easily be dispensed with.

218
Die-Cast Online
http://www.die-cast.com

Die-Cast Online is an extensive resource dedicated to diecast models from all makers and scales. There are five primary sections to this web site, each of which is a valuable resource for any diecast collector or enthusiast. The manufacturing section talks about many diecast manufacturers from around the world and offers links to both the official web sites and a gallery of the manufacturers' models. The descriptions cover history and a general overview of the company.

Another section is collecting, and this lists sources of diecast, tips on collecting, a pricing guide, a booklist and information on how to display your diecast collection, among other things.

The restoring section offers valuable information about the cleaning, retouching, handling and detailing of diecast. Also discussed are the basic tools one will need to accomplish detailing, the pros and cons of detailing and extremely thorough tips on how to make your diecast model ultra-realistic. The other two sections are a model gallery and a links page, both of which are great resources.

219
Diecast Reference Central (Diecast Toy Collectors Association)
http://www.toynutz.com

This site, managed by noted diecast writer Dana Johnson, is one of the best diecast related web sites on the net. There is extensive information about manufacturers, magazines, clubs and other subjects. The site is divided into several sections.

Diecast A–Z offers information on brands, manufacturer overviews and links. There is a list of diecast magazines complete with addresses and links. Another feature of this site is the diecast FAQ section, which includes questions about the real sizes of the various scales used with model cars. There are also links, books for sale, background on Dana Johnson, and an extensive list of U.S. toy dealers and display case makers and retailers complete with links and addresses.

220
eBay
http://www.ebay.com

Everyone heard of the mighty eBay when its initial public stock offering went ballistic in late 1998. While not strictly automobile related, this auction site has a huge automotive section that includes thousands of automotive items for auction by private parties from around North America and occasionally beyond. You can find almost anything here, from complete Rolls-Royce automobiles to grommets for the firewall of a 1961 Chevrolet. Increasingly eBay seems to be the fashionable (and profitable) way to get rid of the things you've been meaning to put out at the next neighborhood garage sale.

221
EWA & Miniature Cars USA
http://www.ewacars.com
http://www.autobooks.com
http://www.automobilia.com

EWA is a one-stop shop for scale cars, books, videos, and related items. It has grown from a local shop located in Green Brook, N.J., to an international shop that carries a large line of automobilia. It offers model photos, newsletters, secure ordering, magazines, CD-ROMs, posters, special sales, featured items, gift certificates, and international ordering. It also issues a paper catalog, some pages from which are posted on the site.

222
***Mobilia* Magazine Online**
http://www.mobilia.com

Mobilia magazine has created a community in which to buy, sell and trade diecast in particular and all automobilia in general. You have to register either as a buyer or a seller to gain access to the site, but registration consists simply of inputting your e-mail address. In January of 1999, the site began to feature a mobilia auction service with over 35,000 items consigned before the grand opening.

Even so, this site offers a great deal of additional content. It enables you to search the classified sections for model or dealer, or to perform a general classified search. The usual subscription information is included as well. There are two main classified sections. One is for toys and models and lists a huge selection of rare and high quality merchandise for sale by private parties and businesses. The other is general automobilia. Here you can find items such as go-karts, hot rod memorabilia, license plates, literature, books and many others. This site also offers the results of auctions to give collectors a feel for what their memorabilia may be worth. There is information about the buyer's guide, links, show and event dates, and how to advertise.

Some of the links on this site do not take you where you would expect them to. Some links took me to the middle of pages, rather than the top, for no apparent reason. Once you get into some sections, you have to click back to the home page to get at the original links because the ones that are on the section pages oftentimes don't work. This is easily fixed, and may indeed be by the time this book is published.

223
MotorBooks
http://www.motorbooks.com

MotorBooks is the online book selling vehicle for MBI Publishing (formerly Motorbooks International). Also included are MBI's imprints Bicycle Books, Classic Railroad Books, TimesPast and Zenith Books. Other offerings include recommendations, monthly features, a search utility, a best-sellers list and critiques.

224
PL8S.COM Magazine
http://www.pl8s.com

License plate collecting is one of those hobbies that anybody can do. That's what makes plates one of the most popular automotive collectibles around. They are easy to get at and numerous, and even the most mundane probably has a history to it. Every enthusiast has at least a couple lying around the shop or even displayed on the wall, and the local drive-in usually has some nailed to the wall. From the old polar bear shaped plates from Alaska to a set off Grandma's Fairmont, plate collecting is something everyone can enjoy. PL8S.COM Magazine offers a glimpse into the world of this hobby and the more specialized areas of plate collecting.

This site is an extensive companion to a magazine by the same name and offers a wealth of information for people who pursue this hobby. There are many photographs of rare and interesting plates such as those from other countries, error plates and others; a book list; terminology and abbreviations related to the hobby; classified ads; plates for sale; a directory of collectors, clubs and publications; links; a schedule of conventions and meets; and last but not least an FAQ section.

225
Primarily Petroliana
http://www.oldgas.com

Primarily Petroliana is a web site dedicated to "bringing gas station antique collectors, dealers, publishers and service providers together for the benefit of all."

This site has a number of features. The sponsor maintains a bookstore in association with Amazon.com that offers many handpicked gas station, petroleum and automotive books, as well as a large directory of oil and gas swap meets and auctions around the country. Also featured on the site are classified ads for gas station collectibles, Gas Station Shop Talk (forums for questions, wanted items, and comments), a list of petro collectors, a list of restored gas stations and displays located at museums and such, and a list of petro resource both on and off-line. The filling station information section offers articles about collecting and history, and there are links to vendors and collectors among others. The link list is long and interesting, featuring many interesting roadside links as well.

226
Road Map Collectors of America
http://www.roadmaps.org

Road Map Collectors of America is an organization that promotes the hobby of map collecting throughout North America and Great Britain. It claims over 300 members and holds an annual meet in Chicago to help collectors and visitors alike with their hobby.

The site consists of several sections, the first of which is "Club Information." This section includes "A Brief History of Road Maps" and a summary of how the hobby has developed over the years. They also provide reprints of their newsletter articles for a small fee. There is information on joining the RMCA, the benefits of joining and so on.

The RMCA also offers a mailing list, "Roadmaps-L," and there is an archive of past and current months. The mailing list is open to everybody, not just RMCA members. It is also offered in digest format. Another interesting feature of the RMCA web site is the "Official Maps Master List," which is "an attempt to catalog all known 'official' state and provincial highway maps (maps produced by state or provincial governments)." The list is arranged by state or province and is quite extensive; each state or province list goes back into the early 1900s at least.

There are stories about road maps and petroleum companies, plus a section in which you can buy and sell maps. There are map dealers, a member wish list, upcoming events, road map links, member services and other features.

227
Strictly Stock.Com
http://www.strictlystock.com

Strictly Stock.Com is a large web site dedicated to those who build and collect scale model automobiles. This web site covers plastic kits, larger diecast (1:18) models, promotional models and model car accessories. The site has a simple framed design and is easy to get around.

The site includes an introduction by Larry A. Greenberg, the editor and webmaster of Strictly Stock.Com. There is also advertising information and other site utilities such as contact information. On the content side, the site contains model kit news, which serves as a place to get info on new model kits; aftermarket news, which acts as a new product showcase for aftermarket accessories such as decal kits and parts; diecast car news, which shows new diecast models that are, or soon will be, available; the Swap Meet, a classified directory; and an e-mail directory of collectors, retailers and other important contacts within the industry. Finally, there is the links section, with a nice collection of related links to other web sites.

Additional Web Sites

228 *Scorchin' Die-Cast* magazine
http://www.scorchin.com

229 Hot Wheels
http://www.hotwheels.com

230 Maisto International, Inc.
http://www.maisto.com

231 Matchbox
http://www.matchbox.com

232 Corgi Classics
http://www.corgi.co.uk

233 Racing Champions
http://www.racingchamps.com

234 Models of Yesteryear
http://www.btinternet.com/~mark.robbins/

235 The National Model Car Builders' Museum
http://www. xmission.com:80/~msgsl/nmcbm/

236 *Plastic Fanatic* magazine
http://www.plasticfanatic.com

237 Motor Racing Models
http://www.motorracingmodels.com

238 Model Motoring, Inc. (HO scale slot cars)
http://www.modelmho.com/

239 Vintage Vending
http://www.vintagevending.com/

240 Tower Hobbies R/C Web Directory
http://www.towerhobbies.com/rcweb.html

241 NORRCA Radio Control Car Racing Organization
http://www.norrca.com

242 nitroRC.com
http://www.nitrorc.com

243 Art & Racing
http://www.art-racing.com

244 CARSoft: Auto Art for Car Fans
http://members.aol.com/carsoft

245 Speed and Beauty Automotive Videos
http://www.speedandbeauty.com

246 Scale Dreams Model Car Detailing
http://www.scaledreams.com

247 Driving Impressions
http://www.drivingimpressions.com

8
COMPREHENSIVE SITES

Comprehensive sites cover a wide range of automotive topics and are generally regarded as the most extensive sites that the Internet has to offer. Often backed by large companies or organizations, these sites offer a wealth of information and shouldn't be passed up.

248
Acceleration Online
http://www.acceleration-online.com

Acceleration Online offers a range of automotive attractions including the unusual feature of dealership reviews. In the dealer reviews section, readers are encouraged to comment on their experiences with car dealers. The selection is limited at the moment but seems to be big in the future.

The site also includes new vehicle reviews that are written by both readers and the author of the site. There are classified ads, a universal message board and a calendar of when car and truck models are due to be restyled or replaced by new models. In addition to all of this is a links section.

249
ALL Automotive
http://www.allautomotive.com

ALL Automotive provides a directory service that helps you find what you're looking for right in your state. Visitors are able to search for new car dealers, used car dealers, tools, and equipment; there is also a parts locator and a service locator. The site includes a special classic car section with club listings, links, and cars and parts for sale. There is also a resources section that includes a number of links and a chat room.

ALL Automotive has undergone some changes over the past year and is better than ever. The site can be confusing sometimes but overall is a nice site with a friendly atmosphere.

250
The Auto Channel
http://www.theautochannel.com

The Auto Channel is an enormous site that covers a great deal of automotive information. The only problem with the Auto Channel is its design. It's graphic-heavy, making it very slow to load, and its layout can be confusing because there are links that shoot all over the place scattered over every page. The amount of information is quite staggering, but you really have to root around in the site to get at all of it. The site is part of a seemingly larger network, so the servers are the same when you jump to different places, which can make it confusing to get a quick reference of where you are. Another annoying problem is that it's too big for a 15-inch monitor.

But, enough of the down side. The Auto Channel offers a plethora of goods—including live cyberchat, new car information, news, motorsports and more. One of its main assets is the quantity of information in each section. The news section includes dozens of articles, both recent and slightly older.

The site is not wasted on frivolity. The media section alone is worth the trip; included are numerous videos, music recordings, news clips, commercial reels and similar items. There are at least a couple hundred offerings here, making it, quite possibly, the most extensive collection of automotive media on the net that is available for free viewing via streaming video. As with most of the Internet, this works best with a fast connection.

251
Auto Fever
http://www.autofever.com

Auto Fever is a large web site that that covers a wide range of automotive topics from classics to new automobiles and everything in between. The web site includes classified ads arranged in several categories such as cars, trucks, classics, antiques, customs, parts, services and RVs. Along with this is daily automotive news, car club links, a bookstore, magazine subscriptions, NASCAR material, weekly racing news, a bulletin board, race schedules, race car art, photos and more.

There is also a muscle car specifications page which includes a large number of muscle cars from the '60s and '70s. The specs include model, year, engine, horsepower (BHP), transmission, torque, axle ratio, curb weight, 0–60 MPH and quarter-mile times. This section includes AMC, Buick, Opel, Chevrolet and Dodge.

252
Auto Trivia
http://www.autotrivia.com

Auto Trivia offers a great trivia challenge in three main sections. You can take challenges based on 1950s, 1960s or 1970s cars. The premise is that if you can answer 20 questions, you really know your automobiles. If you fail to answer five, you get disqualified. If you can do well enough, you can also see you name listed on a special "top scores" page of those who have done well.

Other pages of this simple site are rules and links, and you can add your own question if you think you have a good one. There is also a CD-ROM version of the trivia challenge that should be out by the time this book is printed. The questions are fun and challenging, but they do give you a hint if you feel you should need it. Sometimes the hint is fairly worthless, however.

253
Auto.com — Daily news & reviews
http://www.auto.com

Auto.com is an automotive news service that offers breaking news, industry news, stock updates, auto show coverage, test drives and reviews, forums and more. The coverage is updated daily. The site is fairly simple and easy to use with a well thought out design.

254
Automobiles.Com
http://www.automobiles.com

This site serves as a clearinghouse of sorts for various automotive topics. Its main focus seems to be new and used car buying and related services, with many links to the big names in the online automobile purchasing and ownership sites. The site's design is rather disjointed, but this is a very good place to start looking when you don't really know what you're looking for.

255
The Car Connection
http://www.thecarconnection.com

The Car Connection offers it readers a wealth of interesting articles on all automotive subjects. One could browse and read through the articles for several hours and still have plenty to spare. There are also tons of vehicle reviews. The site includes current news and articles, weekly news briefs, reports on what's new in the industry, links, events, an "on-site" mechanic that answers your questions, an "@ The Wheel" column by Bob Bondurant, spy shots and other tidbits. This site ranks in my top three among article/news sites because of the wealth of current content written by a wide range of authors.

256
Cars & Culture Home Page
http://www.carsandculture.com

This site is exclusively sponsored by Toyota Motor Sales, U.S.A. (http://www.toyota.com) and produced by Time, Inc. In the tradition of well funded web sites, its three content "channels" are gateways to an extensive collection of articles, services and more.

The three featured "channels" are Road Trips, which includes travel information, mapping and routing services, and articles; Auto Culture, which covers anything that relates to cars, culture, people and the reasons why automobiles take such a prominent role in our daily lives and rituals; and Cars & Kids, which covers how children of all ages interact with cars.

The nice thing about this section is that it covers everything from a child's first wheels (pedal cars) to the real thing (a driver's license).

Other minor sections include interactive games (which may require plug-ins or Java), articles and trivia.

257
Detroit News
http://detroitnews.com

Often overlooked by enthusiasts, newspaper sites are often great resources of information, especially when that newspaper happens to be the *Detroit News*. The *Detroit News* hosts perhaps one of the most valuable automotive news sites on the Internet today as it offers an entire realm of services in addition to its excellent worldwide coverage of automotive news. Subsections include Joyrides, a sub-site that is dedicated to hobbyists and enthusiasts of classic and hot rod automobiles. Items of note that can be found in Joyrides include a photo gallery, links, an event calendar and articles regarding classics and customs.

Other features include "Auto Industry" by Dan Howes, an insider report; "Women's Auto Help Center"; road tests of new models by both men and women drivers; excellent photographs; Q&A with the (in)famous Tom & Ray Magliozzi (aka the Tappet Brothers)*; back issues; and links. If you are even remotely interested in what is happening in the automotive industry on a day-to-day basis, this site deserves a bookmark right at the top of your list.

258
eAuto (Everything Automotive)
http://www.eauto.com

The eAuto site offers its visitors a large portfolio of options from which to choose. It offers car buying services, financing services through CarFinance.com, insurance services and more, all at no charge to eAuto viewers. Other sections on the web site are chat, a site of the week and site of the week archives, headline automotive industry news, a guestbook and a very comprehensive directory of automotive web sites, newsgroups and other web resources.

The site's design is slick and simple, but to reach all that it has to offer at once, you have to click on the site directory or use the search. Otherwise it's possible to inadvertently skip over good information as you dig deeper into a specific section.

Services include off-lease car buying services, PrivacyGuard credit reporting and a magazine subscription service through the eAuto news-

*Car Talk *fans should also see the show's own web site, located at www.cars.com.*

stand, offering heavily discounted magazine subscriptions to all of your favorite automobile magazines.

259
GeoCities Motorcity Neighborhood
http://www.geocities.com/MotorCity

Thousands and thousands of automotive and "motor" related sites, all in one place. An entire directory in itself could be devoted to the sites located here. There are a number of good sites, but they are identified by numbers, so it's hard to tell what's what, and the descriptions that people use for their sites are often not very enlightening. GeoCities' main drawback is not in the lack of site descriptions, but in the pop-up ad window that is always fighting the main window for monitor real estate. The ad can be sent behind the main screen but will eventually force itself back into the front. Of course, GeoCities has to pay for its services somehow, but I would prefer to see it done in a different fashion.

GeoCities does not stop at offering reams of web sites, however. It also offers Landmark Sites, which are what GeoCities considers to be the cream of the crop. There are also chat sites and forums.

GeoCities is known for its free web pages. MotorCity consists of a number of "neighborhoods," each with its own specific twist on the main topic. The current neighborhoods include MotorCity, Downs, Flats, Garage, Pit, Speedway and Track. Each one has thousands of sites.

260
The Motoring Network
http://www.themotoringnetwork.com

In a nutshell, at the time of my review, there was nothing here. Every page had an "under construction" sign and no content. The only exception was the gallery, which featured about two dozen photographs of classic automobiles. Empty sections were the Motoring Mall, Programming, Gallery, Main Street (contact information) and Links. The News page did contain a single press release from the Motoring Network stating that it has created an Internet presence. Perhaps the site will be fleshed out soon. It's worth checking back.

261
Off-Road.com
http://www.off-road.com

The Off Road Network is a huge resource for off-road enthusiasts of all types. Whether you're a weekend camper or run the Baja, there will be something for you on this web site. Off-Road.com is not affiliated with *Off-Road* magazine.

Off-Road.com offers more than just automobiles; it also covers dirt-bikes, ATV-Quads and snowmobiles. Almost anything that goes off-road is covered.

The site covers a huge range of topics, and if it is not covered directly by Off-Road.com, one of the network member sites will probably have the 4x4 answers that you're looking for.

There is a large collection of regular articles as well as breaking news on the racing and off-road front. Along with the regular articles there are numerous feature stories on various topics. There are also product reviews. In the Marketplace are a product showcase, a vendor showcase, product reviews, book/video reviews, the Off-Road.com Mall and free classified ads.

The site also contains a bulletin board, stories and folklore, mailing lists, home pages on the network, links, events, trail reports, a photo album, club listings, information on land use issues and off-road technical advice, with several FAQs and how-to tips.

This is a very comprehensive site and is a must-see for any off-road enthusiast.

262
SportUtility/SUV Online
http://www.sportutility.com
http://www.suv.com

SUV online is part of a large network of KII Automotive Group sites (http://www.vmag.com/). KII is a large publisher of electronic content. SUV Online offers SEMA coverage, SUV of the Year Awards, accessory news, reports on what's new in the SUV industry, features, an owner's forum, Camel Trophy coverage and links to other KII sites.

A partial list of the KII network of sites includes the following: America's 4X4 4U Video Magazine (www.4x44u.com); SUV OnLine (www.suv.com); Automotive Catalog Mall (www.catalogs.vmag.com); Show'N Shine OnLine (www.shownshine.com); JJOURNAL (www.jjournal.net); WorkTruck.Com (www.worktruck.com); SUV Network (www.suvnet.com); Ride and Drive (www.rideanddrive.com); HummerNet.Com (www.hummernet.com); LRChronicles (www.lrchronicles.com); AdventureZine (www.adventurezine.com); 4x4 and OffRoad Stores (www.4x4offroad.com); and United Four Wheel Drive Associations Website (www.ufwda.org).

263
Supercars.Net
http://www.supercars.net

Supercars.net offers a large database of vehicle statistics for exotic and high performance automobiles from around the world. Although the site states that "statistics may not be accurate," this is a good source for general specifications for high performance vehicles from recent years and years past.

264
Team.Net
http://www.team.net

Team.Net is a non-profit organization that puts automotive sites and mailing lists on the web. The group, or its membership, maintains a large collection of mailing lists dedicated to various automobiles and automotive topics. A small sample of the mailing lists includes Vintage Race, Sunbeam Tigers, Shop-Talk, Minis, Pre-War British Cars, and Auto-Cross. This is just a sample of the lists that are available. Many of the lists are available in digest form, meaning that you won't get the incredible volume that some of these lists generate, but usually you don't get the opportunity to respond with a digest version.

Team.Net also includes an FTP archive with which you can get access to the mailing list archive, photographs and more.

The primary part of Team.Net is the "Webs." Each Team.Net Web is about a different subject. The current subjects are autocross, museums, British Cars, shop talk, vintage racers and the KTUD Archive. The KTUD Archive is a huge site in its own right.

Each Web contains information about its topic as well as sites, mailing list information and quite a bit more.

Team.Net has a very heavy British/European slant, although there is tons of info on other automotive topics as well.

265
Truckers/Transportation Homepage
http://www.truckers.com

Although this site focuses primarily on trucks, it is included because of its extensive collection of specialized transportation information. The specialized content area is, of course, truckers and trucking throughout the United States. The site features more than 2,500 transportation links, a bulletin board, a chat room, a guestbook, a quote of the day, and Dave's Desk, which acts as a cross between a site history and an editorial.

All of the links are trucking oriented, and include truck stops, diesel price watch, companies, towing, N.A.F.T.A., loads/equipment, food, weather, maps, news and a great deal more.

266
U.S. Auto News
http://www.usautonews.com

U.S. Auto News is a relatively new site that offers a large number of links, both on the web site and via a CD-ROM that contains over 1,600 automotive bookmarks. You can purchase the CD-ROM from the web site. This is an interesting concept that has not been tried before in the automotive sector. Other industries, most notably entertainment, have used the CD-ROM model with some measure of success. It will be interesting to see how it develops over the next several years.

At the time of my visit, the site was very fresh. Many of its content sections, such as headline news, US AutoMail, industry employment, news room and its classified section, were "coming soon." The directory section of the site was fully operational, however, and included a large number of links. The only downside is that none of the links have any sort of description. Their sections include accessories, parts, auto rental, appraisal guides, auto body, racing, clubs and some others. This would be a good site to keep an eye on in the future. If the site does manage to deliver what it promises, it should be very good.

Additional Web Sites

267 Popular Science: Automotive Section
http://www.popsci.com/content/automotive

268 Cars Online
http://www.4cars.com

269 1 Stop Autohobby Info
http://autohobbyist.com

270 AuHo?
http://www.auho.com

271 The Global Automobile Center
http://www.icemall.com/cars/index.html

272 Pit-Stop
http://www.pit-stop.com

273 KTUD Automotive Web
http://www.team.net/www/ktud

274 Driving America
http://www.drivingamerica.com

275 Mark's 4WD Links
http://www.4wdlinks.com

276 Ford Truck Enthusiast Site
http://www.ford-trucks.com

277 Auto Museum
http://www.automuseum.com

9
DRIVING & DESTINATIONS

The fine art of driving has received lots of coverage on the net. Everybody has an opinion on what "good" driving is and how to go about it, and there are a number of sites that are willing to offer you tips.

There are also a lot of sites that cover the essence of driving—getting somewhere. When you drive, you are generally going someplace, even if you don't know where that someplace is. In that light, destination sites are also included on this page.

This chapter covers topics such as driving, destinations, roadside attractions, driving schools, drunk driving, speed limits, speed traps, unsafe driving and related subjects.

278
Ask Mr. Traffic with Kenny Morse
http://www.mrtraffic.com

This rather obnoxious site takes forever and a day to load, and when you do get back from getting your oil changed and tires rotated you will find that it is about 90 percent self-promotion and 10 percent content. Every time I visit this site it seems to crash my system, so I never had a chance to fully explore it.

279
California Drunk Driving — Driver Performance Institutes
http://www.dui.com

This site is a complete reference on DUI in the state of California. Much of the information such as the general FAQs can be extended to other states. Although this is certainly an "anti–DUI" site, the sponsors are sensitive enough to the issue that they present information from both sides of the issue; for example, they provide quite a bit of information on how not to get convicted if you get pulled over, and on the flip side they show pictures of DUI crashes, so the message they present can be a bit confusing.

The site offers DUI education which takes the form of an FAQ section. A list of lawyers who specialize in defending those charged with DUI is provided. There is information about substance abuse in general and, as noted, pictures of severe accidents caused at least in part by impaired drivers. Also included on this site are links, DUI preventative measures, a list of DUI schools in California, tips on what you should do if you have gotten arrested for DUI and what the various punishments could be if you are convicted.

Perhaps the greatest asset this site has to offer is the DUI Library, which is a very large collection of articles and information on DUI and alcohol issues. The library contains articles from newspapers and magazines detailing DUI legislation, accidents and statistics.

280
Campaign Against Drunk Driving (CADD)
http://www.drunkdriving.com

CADD's mission is to "eliminate drunk driving as a leading cause of death of young Americans." CADD's plan to achieve this goal is through severe legislation against drunk drivers, and the group's web site includes the history of the organization, links, information and relevant statistics to aid this cause. The site also includes articles from various sources about the increase in drunk driving deaths in the United States.

281
Car Guys, Inc.
http://www.carguys.com

This company provides on-track high performance driver education programs located in Roanoke, Va., and serves the southeastern United States. The site includes a schedule, FAQs, sign-up, links and more. In this program, you supply everything, including the vehicle.

282
Drive Safer America
http://www.drivesaferamerica.com

Drive Safer America is a nice site dealing with all facets of driving safety. The site is maintained by Continental Teves, a company that develops and manufactures automotive safety systems. The primary focus of this site is on ABS brakes, but there is quite a bit of other content as well.

There is a news and events section that shows news releases and information about the site's newsletter such as how to get it mailed to you and how to get back issues. You can also read the current issue and back issues online. The newsletter includes a number of articles on various automotive topics, but primarily safety concerns. There are tips on year-round system-by-system vehicle maintenance as well as on how to drive more safely.

Driving statistics for the United States are also included on this site. The statistics are mainly on fatal crashes divided up by general cause and environment. In this section you will also find links to other automotive safety sites.

Since the Continental Teves company manufactures ABS, there is a great deal of information about ABS brakes including a very good Q&A section covering basic and advanced issues. There is also an ABS survey that readers can fill out.

283
Drive 2000
http://www.driving.daelnet.co.uk

Drive 2000 is a web site dedicated to safe driving in the U.K. It is sponsored, written and designed by Chris Parker, a driving instructor.

Sections of the site includes information on the "L" test. In the U.K., young drivers are required to take an "L" test to get their provisional license, which is the equivalent of a probationary license in the United States. The "L" designation comes from the special plates that are displayed on the young driver's vehicle. This specific site includes sample questions on the written test and other general information about the test as a whole.

There is a driver's information center, which gives drivers of all levels tips on road rage, what to do in an accident, safety, buying a used car, drinking and driving, driving in the fog and other topics of interest to drivers. Visitors can also take advantage of the advanced driver index that gives more details on advanced driving schools and institutes within the U.K.

Drive 2000 also includes a large collection of driving related links from around the world and a photo album of crash scenes caused by various means such as alcohol and negligence. Also be sure to check out the driving news, and if you need to learn how to drive or brush up on your technique, there is a section where you can find a good driving instructor in your area.

284
DRIVE-NET
http://www.drive-net.com

A resource for drivers of all levels of expertise. Visitors will find all the basics for beginners as well as techniques for the expert driver.

285
Enjoy the Road (Route 66)
http://www.route66.com

There is only one "Mother Road," and that road is classic Route 66 from Chicago to Los Angeles. This site is one of the many that are dedicated to old Route 66. There is a host of sections including a very detailed history of the historic route. This historical information is probably some of the Internet's best on old Route 66. Another section talks about the creators of the site, TransCom Global, Ltd., and there is a news section that includes happenings on Route 66, current developments, restoration projects by various Route 66 enthusiast groups, motor tours and more.

286
Flat Out
http://www.tridentgroup.com/speed.htm

I first visited Flat Out several months before returning to review it for this book, and did it change! It used to have my vote for best web site title with the name "Flat Out 'Til You See God ... Then Brake!" but now it's been toned down to simply "Flat Out." The site certainly is dedicated to driving — specifically driving fast.

Included within its pages are fast road stories, where the best fast roads are and other news. The news section covers how states deal with speed limits, and includes editorials, commentary on radar detector issues and more.

Flat Out is a small part of a large, very diverse non-automotive site.

287
How to Drive Like a Moron
http://members.aol.com/doggiesnot

This is one of the more interesting and entertaining sites on the net, especially if you've just had a bad day on the freeway. The numerous sections include tips on passing, general driving, highways, accidents, parking lots, back seat drivers, using headlights and other topics. There are hundreds of tips on becoming a "Moron Driver" and you can even issue a "summons" to a moron driver in the form of a printable "ticket" to place on the offender's automobile. Also, report a moron and add them to the list of moron drivers currently found on the site.

288
MADD On-Line
http://www.madd.org

Mothers Against Drunk Driving is a coalition of people who have banded together to help educate and inform people about the dangers of drunk driving. MADD On-Line offers a huge amount of information that does just that. MADD offers online victim tributes, information on the group's many programs, public policy notes, a local chapter locator, chat, *DRIVEN* magazine, information on supporting MADD and more. Perhaps one of the most valuable pieces of information that MADD offers is its statistical data. It's hard to find another comprehensive collection of information in one spot. Data include fatalities by holiday and state, general statistics, information broken down by racial divides, and BAC (blood alcohol content) levels and conversion charts. The site also features facts about drinking and driving and dispels many of the "myths" associated with driving while being intoxicated.

Overall, this site does what it is meant to extremely well and is presented in a well thought out design that offers easy navigation and readability.

289
NHTSA — National Highway Traffic Safety Administration
http://www.nhtsa.dot.gov

Perhaps the ultimate in safety advocation, the NHTSA is the U.S. Department of Transportation's highway safety organization. This site includes a massive amount of information on automobile safety of all kinds, with text on air bags, advanced air bags, child safety, an Auto Safety Hotline (1-888-DASH-2-DOT), vehicle testing results, regulations and standards info, recognized and suspected safety problems, recalls, tech bulletins, investigations, complaint info and more. This is just a scratch on the surface.

Driver performance, injury prevention and outreach programs are a few of the site's other subjects. The site also includes the National Driver Register, a service with which qualified individuals and organizations can get information on drivers who have had their licenses revoked or suspended or have been convicted of serious traffic violations. Another feature is a listing of DOT offices and phone numbers in every state.

290
Reasonable Drivers Unanimous
http://sunsite.unc.edu/rdu

This site, by Kevin Atkinson, is dedicated to the reasonable allocation of speed limits around the United States. This is a large and well presented site, although the argument is rather one-sided (but offers a superb source of information on why speed limits should be lowered).

Although the entry page is somewhat difficult to read and you are required to fill out an anonymous form, the rest of the site is easy to use and is presented free of graphics to provide visitors with a simple interface to the information provided.

RDU offers its visitors information about speed limits, why they are set the way they are, the role of insurance companies and the courtrooms in determining speed limits, statistics on raising and lowering limits, the retelling of driving adventures, message boards, commentary, "secrets" about speed limits, links, commentary on driver's education, tips on driving courtesy and skills, a guestbook and more! As you can see, this is a rather comprehensive site when it comes to speed limit issues.

291
Roadside America
http://www.roadsideamerica.com

Roadside America, billed as "Your Online Guide to Offbeat Attractions," is one of those sites that you can spend hours wandering in. It has so much unique and interesting information, it's hard to know where to start, and more is being added all the time. Roadside America specializes in the unusual, the bizarre and the simply strange. From the world's largest fiberglass fish to museums of the macabre, these are the ultimate in roadside attractions we all know and love from our overland trips.

Simply amazing is a good description of the types of things you'll find on Roadside America. There a "sight of the week" that showcases one unusual attraction of note. Navigation is easy with the "Electric Map," which you can use to browse state-by-state listings of attractions. Chances are there is at least one bizarre attraction within an hour of where you live, perhaps even unknown to you.

You can also visit the souvenir hut, where you can buy T-shirts, *Roadside America: The Book*, and a large list of books that relate to the Roadside America theme. Be sure to visit the Vortex, a catch-all of miscellaneous attractions.

The design of this site is easy at first, but then you can get lost easily. This doesn't bother me in in the slightest because each page has links to other great pages. It helps reinforce the "hall of mirrors" feel this site has. It's hard to care where the home page is when you're taking a peek at a stuffed albino squirrel riding a motorcycle.

292
The Speedtrap Registry
http://www.speedtrap.com

The Speedtrap Registry, founded in February of 1995, is one of the legends of the Internet. It is probably one of the most linked-to and visited automotive sites on the net. The site is divided up into five distinct sections. The "About" section includes general information about the site and its creator, Andrew Warner.

The "Other" info section includes a link or two, radar detector laws by state, and a "cop car registry" detailing what types of police cars are used on a state by state basis.

Two sections form the main focus of the site. One is the U.S. Speedtraps section, which includes a state-by-state overview of speedtraps as reported by drivers. Each trap is detailed by location, average cost of ticket, type of police car used, frequency, a map and other data. There are numerous speedtraps for each state listed, including everything from small town cops to the state patrol. The other section covers foreign speed traps. These are listed by country and are more like general overviews than specific listings as with the U.S. traps.

The last section is how to add a speed trap to the directory. All in all this is a well done and easy-to-use site.

293
Tread Lightly!
http://www.treadlightly.org

The Tread Lightly! program is designed to promote the responsible use of the outdoors during recreational activity, including 4x4 activities. This web site details the program and offers merchandise, some history on the program and other material.

Additional Web Sites

294 Rand McNally Online
http://www.randmcnally.com

295 Driveways of the Rich and Famous
http://www.driveways.com

296 Driving On Line
http://www.driving.co.uk

297 MapBlast!
http://www.mapblast.com

298 Dollar Rent-a-Car Great Drives
http://www.dollarcar.com/grtdrive.html

299 us70east.com
http://www.us70east.com

300 John Farlam's Advanced Driving
http://www.driving-skills.demon.co.uk

301 America's Driving Force
http://www.americasdrivingforce.com

302 Drivers.com
http://www.drivers.com

10
EZINES & PUBLICATIONS

There are four "heavy hitters" in the new automobile publication list for the United States: Motor Trend, Road & Track, Car and Driver *and* Automobile *magazines. These publications have gone full force onto the net, to the benefit of the consumer and enthusiast, and have created mega-sites filled with information. These automobile magazines are primarily geared to the new-car buyer and the enthusiast.*

In addition to these mega-sites, there are numerous sites dedicated to specialty or less widely known magazines. These sites also offer a wealth of information.

303
African American on Wheels (Automag)
http://www.automag.com

African American on Wheels is an online magazine dedicated to African American new car buyers. This site also contains information on *Automag*, a quarterly publication dedicated to African American automobile interests. It features a commentary on new automobiles, and these commentaries are archived so you can read past articles. A large list of new auto show dates from around the United States, an index of current articles in *Automag*, and full of text of selected articles are posted on this web site. There is also an archive of past issues. Although the magazine and web site are geared toward African Americans, the articles are informative and are of interest to everyone.

304
Autobuzz
http://www.autobuzz.com

Autobuzz is a large e-magazine dedicated to import performance cars. The design is well thought out, and a simple, compact navigation structure makes getting around a snap. *Autobuzz* covers events with a calendar and additional information is presented when available.

The site features a performance shop list organized by state and a mailing list that enables subscribers to be updated on events, site updates, contests and more. In order to get at all the information, you need to sign up for free membership. Some great features are an online technical forum, links, contests and a buy/sell area with domestic and import cars. Also featured are the "Auto Files," where one specific car is always featured. There are message boards, too.

305
AutoExpress
http://www.autoexpress.co.uk

AutoExpress is one of the best e-magazines coming out of the U.K., and its coverage is almost exclusively British. The only gripe I have with this site is that you have to register to get in. The registration can be a clumsy process, but once you've registered you can bookmark the home page and never have to register or "log-on" again. The registration involves giving your name and e-mail address and answering a couple of short questions, but it's well worth the trouble to get at all the great material. Another small annoyance is that the site is too large to fit on an average 15-inch screen so it bleeds off to the right and the bottom. You have to expand your browser to its maximum size even to see that there is a "spy shots" link; otherwise you'd miss it altogether. Finally, the site is a bit graphics intensive, so those with slow connections beware. Design aside, the rest of the site is outstanding. The news sections are current and well-written and cover things that U.S.–centric magazines don't, such as automakers that don't sell their goods in the United States (and there are a lot of very nice automobiles that never see U.S. soil). Visitors can also access a used car price index, previews, road tests, the previously mentioned spy shots of factory mules (a "mule" is a test automobile that is in the pre-production stage and is often one of a kind), links and other features. The news section is in headline format, with a short paragraph about each article, so you can scan before you jump into the article itself.

306
***Automobile* Magazine Online**
http://www.automobilemag.com

Automobile magazine hosts this excellent site that contains scheduled chat, previews of new spy shots, previews of upcoming automobiles, breaking news, message boards, archives, links, a bookstore, classified ads, event coverage and listings, industry news, a buyer's guide — what else could you ask for on one site?

The site's navigation is simple with expanding menus that let you dig deeper into the site without getting lost or giving up the opportunity to jump to any other page.

The buyer's guide is organized by vehicle body style to help you find what you want. Making things easy to find is something that many sites forget about somewhere in the development process, which is really unfortunate. The buyer's guide also features a questionnaire to help you decide what type of vehicle would fit your lifestyle. One excellent feature is the "compare two cars" section, where you can make your top two choices go head-to-head.

An Amazon.com affiliated bookstore is also presented in usable fashion. It combines the advantages of *Automobile* magazine's expertise with the competitive pricing of Amazon.com.

The archive lists a mixed bag of articles, road trips and sneak previews from the pages of the magazine itself. Also featured are Editor's Site Picks with a few of the best auto web sites listed for you to check out. There is a large list of general automotive links to be found. *Automobile* Magazine Online also features a free e-mail newsletter that you can subscribe to. There is the usual industry news commonly found on such sites, too.

In summary, *Automobile* Magazine Online brings the best of its already excellent publication into a tour de force web site that will ensure a bookmark right at the top of the visitor's list.

307
Automobile Quarterly
http://www.autoquarterly.com

Anybody who is serious about the classic car hobby has at least paged through a few issues of *AQ*. It is a hardbound book that is published quarterly and includes a great deal of information on vintage and classic automobiles with the occasional newer car thrown in for good measure. The articles are historically accurate, well written and accompanied by a host of excellent full-color photographs. The web site offers a taste of what you will find in each print edition of *AQ*, featuring an article form a recent issue. The articles are usually very long, informative and dedicated to some historical aspect of the automobile. A "free stuff" section offers a quiz, and you get a prize if you answer it correctly. The site also offers the usual subscription information and merchandise such as back issues, books, models and postcards. The site is relatively small and easy to navigate.

308
***The Automotive Insider* Magazine**
http://www.auto-insider.com

This is a very simple, virtually text-only site mostly concerning automotive auctions. Some of the pages produce error messages.

309
Automotive Week
http://www.auto-week.com

Automotive Week is a weekly newsletter covering the aftermarket industry and targeting aftermarket executives. The web site offers a taste of information on its home page, but after you get past the home page, the general informative value drops off sharply as the site mainly details what the newsletter has to offer subscribers. The information that the site does supply consists of a sample of the classified section, links, how to advertise in the publication, a sample newsletter from a couple of years back, aftermarket association links, story headlines, back issue information and a bit more. This is mainly a large advertisement for the publication, but you can find some interesting information on the site. The targeted audience of this publication are those that are interested in the "nuts & bolts" of the aftermarket industry.

310
AutoWeek Online
http://www.autoweek.com

AutoWeek's web site covers the current issue, listing the table of contents, classified ads and an ePoll. The "About *AutoWeek*" section includes a gallery of covers, a summary of what *AutoWeek* covers, an editorial calendar and rate cards for advertising. Subscription and back issue information, contact information and a section covering motorsports and collector cars round out the site.

The motorsports section includes a schedule of events, TV listings and other items. The "Scenic Route" section provides advertiser links and collector car event listings, among other bits. There is an extensive list of collector car events ranging from vintage shows to hot rod shows. *AutoWeek* is one the industry's premier publications and has the benefit of getting a jump on the big monthly magazines.

311
Car and Driver
http://www.caranddriver.com

Car and Driver, as befits one of the major magazines on the net, gives its viewers a look inside its pages along with some other great content. The site as a whole is keyword searchable, but a series of animated ads in a purely advertising-based frame on the bottom of the site is an unwelcome distraction. However, advertising is the bread and butter of these publications and are a forever ingrained part of commercial web sites.

Car and Driver offers several key content areas. These include "Top Stories," featuring articles about vehicles and other things of note in the auto industry; "Road Tests," with current road test information along with some model previews; "Buyer's Guide," covering vehicles going back about three years or so and searchable by manufacturer, vehicle type, price and year.

Other areas included are: "Car Shows," giving information on major recent or upcoming car shows; "News," with daily articles on breaking and current industry events; "Opinions," with editorials by your favorite *C&D* editors; "Then and Now," a comparison of vehicles currently on the market their namesakes of years past; "Concept Cars," giving an inside look at concept cars from all the makers; "Gear," with information on new aftermarket products; "Subscriptions"; "Store," offering books and *C&D* merchandise; and "Site News," detailing changes to the site itself.

312
Car and Truck News
http://www.car-truck.com

If there is a piece of Chrysler related news that you want to know about, this is the place to look. *Car and Truck News* is dedicated wholly to the Chrysler Corporation and its automobiles, though it is in no official way affiliated with Chrysler. The site features such items as a current year model guide, concept cars, racing news, a listing of manufacturers on the web, rumors, automobile reviews, breaking Chrysler news, and first drive reports. The "breaking news" section is second to none, often beating even such publications as *AutoWeek* with emerging news.

313
***Car Collector* Online**
http://www.carcollector.com

Car Collector magazine is one publication that believes in giving you something on its web site other than an address to send your subscription payment to. Another unusual thing about *Car Collector*'s web site is that it covers both modified and original cars, making little distinction between the two, in contrast to most other organizations. *Car Collector*'s web site offers the visitor a cornucopia of classic car information as well as some general industry tidbits. The site boasts a rather large "shopper" section consisting of classified ads, catalog showcase, marketplace and "The Auto Mall." All of this is supplemented by a new products section with review.

Other regular departments include restoration tips, readers' letters and "Reader's Garage," a section that highlights readers' automobiles. Almost all of *Collector Car*'s previous articles and features are archived, giving more than what's on the surface. A section called "Hotwire" gives the visitor access to auto industry and car collector headlines, and there is a directory of both collector car events and car clubs. There is, of course, the obligatory subscription information page, but the site solicits your visits in a tasteful and nonintrusive way.

314
CarMag
http://www.carmag.co.jp

CarMag is written for readers in Japan and does not offer an alternate English version. It appears to contain quite a bit of information.

315
Cars & Parts Magazine
http://www.carsandparts.com

Cars & Parts magazine is dedicated to providing the serious collector car enthusiast with a venue in which to buy and sell classic cars and parts.

The web site offers its visitors a taste of what the magazine holds. There is a catalog showroom displaying catalogs from various retailers and advertisers. There is also a page of links and information on *Cars & Parts Corvette*, a specialized version of *Cars & Parts* Magazine.

You can search some of the magazine's ads or browse the Collector Car Corral, Classified Word Ads, the Calendar of Events and a Vendor Locator. There is the usual subscription information and advertiser information as well as a small archive of classic car photographs.

Another feature of this web site is a bookstore, offering a selection of books, ID guides and related items that you can order from the web site.

316
CARtoday.com
http://www.carmag.com

CARtoday.com is a large web site that covers Southern Africa. It offers readers a huge number of resources. All of the subjects are relative to Southern Africa and all of the content is in English, but much of the reading will be of interest to readers from around the globe.

Sections include the latest industry news, a news archive, international job search, emergency service information, links and a bookstore. A buyer's guide includes prices, specifications, finance and insurance information and several cost/payment calculators that offer loan payments, fringe benefit tax and other costs of owning an automobile in Southern Africa.

The enthusiast section covers classics, clubs in the area, 4x4s, technology and various other subjects. In addition, there is a motorsports section that currently covers both Formula 1 and general motorsports in Southern Africa.

Finally, the games section offers reviews, tips, hints and more about automobile related games — specifically racing games such as Need for Speed III by Electronic Arts (http://www.nfs3.com) and Gran Turismo by Sony (http://www.granturismo.com — Unofficial Page). There is also a good section dedicated to model cars of all types and scales. There are numerous pictures and coverage of scale model events.

317
Carworld UK
http://www.carworld.co.uk

Carworld is a site that allows users to search the U.K. for new and used automobiles located at dealers around the country. It also has some other services of note.

Carworld UK offers links to British motoring associations and clubs, and its medium-sized list of car clubs covers a wide range of clubs. Carworld UK also offers an auction locator organized geographically by 10 regions of the U.K. including Scotland, Wales, North West, West England, South Central, South East, Thames, East Anglia, Central and North East. The auctions are also categorized into groupings of BCA Actions, CMA Group, Eastbourne Car Auctions, Motor Auction Consortium, National Car Auctions and SCA Auctioneers. Visitors are able to perform a car search for specific automobiles from new and used car dealers by the same geographic locations listed above. There are also directories for equipment and accessories, rentals, services and manufacturers.

318
Classic Motor Monthly
http://www.classicmotor.co.uk

The U.K.–based *Classic Motor Monthly* On-Line can be viewed either with or without frames, which earns it brownie points from those who don't like frames, but on the down side it loads rather slowly. This large site has quite a few things happening. The design is somewhat overwhelming, with bold images and gobs of text about diverse classic automobile topics. This is one of those sites you have to digest slowly.

The Off-Line section is an overview of the current print issue, and there are archives containing articles from past issues. Books and videos can be ordered from a secure web page and there is a large listing of museums located through the U.K.

Classic Motor Monthly On-Line also offers samples from the magazine's "Classic-Fieds" ads, which include vehicles, spares, toys, literature, automobilia, services and other items. There is a wide range of automobilia for sale through this service.

The site also features a large list of classic, vintage and veteran car clubs, a links page, an events listing, news, letters and subscription information.

319
***Cruisin' Times* Magazine**
http://www.cruisintimes.com

Cruisin' Times magazine is published in Texas and Ohio and is a quickly growing classic and hot rod publication. The web site offers information about the magazine, but there is also a good amount of material unique to the web site. You can sign the *Cruisin' Times* guestbook, fill out the survey, join the mailing list, browse the list of upcoming Texas events or list your event.

Visitors can order featured products from the Cruisin' Products page. The featured product at the time of my visit was a Route 66 Duffle Bag. There are Texas–based classified ads and a services page; the latter lists ad rates and links to various services, primarily in the state of Texas.

There is information on the weekly Street Meet and cruise nights, as well as a club listing. You can also get information on getting your vehicle in Texas movies and commercials, plus updates on legislation. In addition to various other features, there is of course information on how to subscribe to the print magazine.

320
***DRIVE*! On-line**
http://www.driveonline.com

This is the companion site to *DRIVE!* magazine, the focus of which is the listing of national, regional and local automotive events dealing mainly with classic cars, hot rods, customs and such. The magazine and web site offer a lot more than this, however. The web site includes subscription information and a table of contents of the current issue of *DRIVE!*, and the web site's own calendar of events, which you can submit your event to. The web site also gives viewers the chance to win some free stuff, offers highlights of the past issues of *DRIVE!* and has other features such as stories, links, classified ads and articles by such rodding luminaries as Boyd Coddington, Ed "Big Daddy" Roth, Ken "Posies" Fenical and others.

There is also a page about *Team DRIVE!*, which is a club that offers special benefits to its members. This is just a small part of the huge amount of information that the *DRIVE!* On-line site offers it's readers.

321
Driving & Style
http://www.drivingandstyle.com

Driving & Style offers numerous articles and pictorials. A publisher's letter provides commentary on a specific subject that changes on a regular basis. Reader's Forum, a Q&A with columnist Jim Grant of "Let's Talk Cars," answers readers' questions. The site features articles on new cars plus sneak peeks at upcoming models and pictorials of classic cars. The collection is quite extensive. The "lifestyles" section includes reviews on books, movies and music that are not necessarily auto related. *Driving & Style* also offers CARtoons, an article archive and some specialized member services such as premium news.

322

Motor Trend

http://www.motortrend.com

Motor Trend, like many other publications, has found that keeping content online is a fantastic way to build readership loyalty. Can't find that specific article in your four foot high stack of back issues? Well, no problem, just click on over to *Motor Trend*'s home on the web and you have a massive resource of information right at your fingertips.

Motor Trend keeps a fairly extensive archive of features, car care tips, performance trends and other articles on its web site in an easy-to-use format that allows you to jump around freely throughout the site. But that's certainly not all that *Motor Trend* has up its electronic sleeves. Also featured are a list of links, a primary feature, auto news, live chat, buying and leasing information, a marketplace, multimedia clips, car of the year award articles, information on Motor Trend TV, classified ads and other items.

The site is easy to navigate and offers a table of contents, a search feature and a help button in case all else fails.

Motor Trend's CarWizard is a unique feature that allows visitors to browse new and used car data, leasing info, insurance quotes, and free car quotes from Autobytel.com quickly and easily. There is also credit information and other items that relate to buying and owning your next automobile.

The multimedia archive contains a photo gallery, video gallery, wallpaper, slide shows, auto shows and more. The sheer number of articles and features makes this site a can't miss stop on the information superhighway.

323

Nutz & Boltz

http://www.motorminute.com

This is a companion site to the *Nutz & Boltz Newsletter*. There is detailed information on what the newsletter provides and the opportunity to join the *Nutz & Boltz* mailing list.

Currently *Nutz & Boltz* offers two major subscription based services.

There is the newsletter, which is "devoted to all transportation issues" and is sent monthly, and the special program, which provides subscribers with a one year membership in the Nutz and Boltz Club, a lube oil analysis kit, a carbon monoxide detector, a key tag finder, a list of secret warranties (service bulletins) or so-called "silent recalls" and other benefits. Full details are available on the web site.

You can listen to the *Nutz & Boltz* radio show online, currently with RealAudio. *Nutz & Boltz* features a radio show that is on WJFK (1300AM) in Baltimore. There is also an archive that features current shows along with approximately four other shows.

Another feature is the Motor Minute, which is a small, often humorous or enlightening tidbit or cartoon on transportation.

Nutz & Boltz also offers a Car Care Tip of the Week, a guestbook, links and an overview of past issues.

324
Ride&Drive
http://www.rideanddrive.com

Ride&Drive is a large, well executed e-magazine that offers a host of valuable and interesting subjects for automotive enthusiasts to browse. It provides general automotive bulletin boards, links, books for sale, and an image archive claiming to hold over 100,000 images from advertising, photography, posters and catalogs (most of which are available to license). There are several galleries in the archive, and the images range from very early automobiles to modern day cars. There are also a few non-automotive related images. The site also has features that change regularly and a large fun and games section that includes "guess the photo" games and other fun interactive activities such as jokes and humor. Featured at the site is industry news, road tests of new cars, trucks and SUVs, buyer's guides and auto show coverage. One of the more interesting categories is the "Design Disasters" area, which details such cars as the Edsel and other more recent design flops.

325
***Road & Track* Online**
http://www.roadandtrack.com

This publication is owned by the same company that owns *Car and Driver* (Hachette Filipacchi Magazines), so you can expect some of the same. *Road & Track* does, however, offer its visitors a decidedly unique looking web site. It features top stories, first looks at upcoming new autos, road trip reports, news and technical advice. There are also letters to the editor, book reviews and subscription information.

The Road Trip section brings the reader information about new vehicles as well as the road trips the editors and writers took with the vehicles. These articles can often give a potential buyer insight into the usability and quirks of a specific automobile. The Open Road section offers coverage of off-road vehicles, trucks and SUVs. The News section talks about what is happening currently and historically in the automotive industry. This section covers other interesting automotive topics including people, places, vintage automobiles and more. There is some technical information as well that has to do exclusively with new automobiles.

Road & Track also offers a feedback page, classified ads and a buyer's guide for the most recent model year. Navigation is hindered by the fact that the web site offers no less than five major clickable areas, and contents are spread somewhat randomly through the five areas. After visiting the site for a while, you get used to it and take it in stride, but beginners can almost miss entire sections because the buttons blend in so well with the design. The entire web site is searchable by keyword.

326
The Special Car Journal

http://www.specialcar.com

The Special Car Journal is a magazine that specializes in classic, exotic and sports cars. Its web site offers many of the same services that the print publication does. There are over 15,000 ads in the classified section and the site was offering free photo ads at the time of my visit. In addition, there is a "yellow pages" directory of over 550 links and other miscellaneous features.

There are reviews of new cars and an advertiser's gallery, where 75 dealers have collected to showcase their online catalogs. There is also a large archive of past articles and issues and coverage of auto shows, especially the high-end concours d'élégance shows held around the world.

If you are familiar with the print version of the *Special Car Journal*, you can find much of the same content on the web site.

327
WheelBase

http://www.wheelbase.com

WheelBase is an extremely simple web site that offers headlines, articles, editorials, features and similar material, all in a straightforward format. Each of the six main sections includes a simple but very large list of links, and each link leads to an article or other feature. The six main sections are motorsports, technology, industry reports, government, opinion and an "About *WheelBase*" section. There is a lot of good reading here if you don't mind a rather dry interface. This design makes it quick, but a little stark. If you're looking for articles or editorials on the above topics, this is the place to look.

Additional Web Sites

328 *The Rodder's Journal*
http://www.roddersjournal.com

329 *duPont Registry*
http://www.dupontregistry.com

330 *Top Gear*
http://www.topgear.com

331 CSKpub: Muscle Car Magazines
http://www.cskpub.com/links.html

332 *Deals on Wheels*
http://www.dealsonwheels.com

333 *AutoFan*
http://www.autofan.com

334 *Auto Gallery* magazine
http://www.autogallerymag.com

335 The Petersen Companies, Inc.
http://www.d-p-g.com

336 *The Mustang Works* Online
http://www.mustangworks.com

337 *Victory Lane* magazine
http://www.victorylane.com

338 Motor Publications
http://www.motor.com

339 *Automotive Body Repair News*
http://www.abrn.com

340 Babcox Publications
http://www.babcox.com

11
PERSONAL SITES

Due to the free-range nature of the Internet, personal sites are often put up by people with an interest in a specific year, make or model of automobile. There are a few, however, that cover a huge array of topics and are every bit as good as sites maintained by corporations.

Personal sites as a group are less stable than corporately sponsored sites, their content and very existence more subject to change without notice. The nature of personal sites causes them to move around on occasion — many stay at the same location for years, but others move on a regular basis. Don't be surprised if these links don't always take you where you expect them to. I have attempted to select only sites that I know have been at the same location for an extended period of time.

The topics represented in this chapter will range from supercars to classics to racing, and each of the sites listed presents some sort of valuable or unique information for the enthusiast or even the casual web surfer.

341
AutoZine
http://home.netvigator.com/~europa

Simply amazing. Those two words alone describe this site well. Mark Wan, a resident of Hong Kong, has created a huge comprehensive database of automotive information. Noticing what many others have seen, that most major automotive media outlets focus almost exclusively on the U.S. market, Wan created his own automotive supersite — AutoZine.

The site holds approximately 375 articles on individual automobiles. Almost every manufacturer on the globe is represented and detailed in the manufacturers section, and Wan has commentary on luminaries in the industry and those he feels have made an impact on the industry. Race car drivers, designers and executives are covered.

Wan also offers technical data, a compilation of the best of AutoZine, links and tons of miscellaneous articles covering everything from the McLaren F1 to technological developments over the past 100 years. AutoZine is one of the most comprehensive, well-presented, non-commercial sites on the net. And amazingly, there is not one shred of advertising on the entire site. My hat is off to Mark Wan.

342
Boulder Bob's Roadster Page
http://www.gohotrods.com

Boulder Bob offers an inside look into the makings of his sharp little 1929 Ford roadster. The site doesn't stop there, though; it includes numerous pics of the '29 as well as other hod rods, a bit of hot rod and street rod events information and photos of several years of the Americruise Tour. The details on the '29 consist of what was done to it and who did it and some trials and tribulations that happened along the way.

There is also a page dedicated to 1946–48 Fords in general and Boulder Bob's '46 rod known only as "The Coupe." The page on "The Coupe" also details what was done to the car and who did it with some wonderful photographs of this wicked-looking ride. There are also pictures of some readers' '46–'48 Fords as well.

Another section that is worth a visit is the links page. Boulder Bob has established a great list of street rodder links as well as some non-rod links thrown in for good measure. As with most personal home pages, there are sporadic links to other places of interest. The page is well presented and loads fairly quickly for the number of graphics.

There is background music, which some people like and some people don't, but Boulder Bob gives the reader the choice of shutting it off, which gives the best of both worlds.

343
Cars of Yesterday
http://www.carsofyesterday.com

This site is placed with the personal pages because even though you can buy and sell cars here, the most distinctive feature is the personal side of it, the photo album. It alone is worth the visit.

Cars of Yesterday is a place where you can buy or sell a classic car. There is also a Photo Album of classics which acts as a scrapbook because it contains other items of interest. It details the collecting habits of the creator of the site, Richard Wilkie, Jr., and is really a very good page all by itself. There are three galleries of photographs here.

344
Classic Rods (formerly *Street Rodders Paradise*)
http://www.classicrods.com

When it was known as Street Rodders Paradise, this was a very good site. When I visited under its new name, however, I was unable to get in. The page loaded and described the site, but there was no way to continue into the rest of the site. It is included here on the assumption that this problem is temporary.

345
Ford Customline
http://www.bitcon.no/~gunnar/customline.html

Ford Customline is a web site dedicated to everything Customline from Ford. The Customline name first adorned Ford vehicles in the early 1950s and is still used today on Ford's conversion vans.

There are numerous sections including information on classic and vintage Fords between 1930 and 1960, as well as the modern vans. There is also a photo gallery.

The best part of this extensive web site is the Customline Forum, featuring hundreds of Customline and general Ford related posts covering all manner of topics.

346
Frank's Land Yacht Marina
http://www.voicenet.com/~perches/landycht.html

This fittingly huge site is dedicated to "land yachts" in general and

Cadillac in particular. There are sections for "ships," "cargo ships" (station wagons), "luxury liners" (Cadillac, Lincoln, Imperial, Packard), "cabin cruisers" (Buicks, Oldsmobiles, Chevrolet, Ford, Studebaker, Chrysler and others), "speedboats" (AMX, Buick Riviera, GS, Regal, Chrysler 300, GTO, Impala, Thunderbird), "lifeboats" (small cars, including Crosley, Nash, Subaru and others), and "the foreign fleet" (Trabant, Renault, Morgan, Mercedes, BMW and others).

The site is sprinkled with great photos and essential services as a list of links to other sites. But the way in which it is presented is great. There is also a news and features page that includes information on what is new on the Land Yacht Marina. There is even some information on the S.S. *United States*, the "greatest American ocean liner of all time," which is bigger and more powerful than the *Titanic* ever was. The "Big U" has sat in mothballs since 1969, all but an empty shell and quietly awaiting its fate. On this page you will also find special links to the "Boatmobile," restoration shops, a collection of car billboards, Carhenge and lots more.

347
G. McDowell's Auto Hobby Page
http://carnut.com

George McDowell has created a large site dedicated to the automotive hobby. Included within its pages are pictures of cars McDowell has owned and the numerous cars he currently owns. There are many good nostalgic photos on this site.

There is information about Chrysler's much celebrated, although never-to-be, 1964 Turbine Car including a couple of good pictures and stories of what happened to the 50 cars that were produced. Also there are the usual links; a scheduled chat session; a guestbook; a large directory of street rod vendors that includes addresses and phone numbers of dozens, if not hundreds, of vendors; some cars for sale; pictures of cars that McDowell's friends own; event listings; and various other goodies.

However, no matter how nice all of the above may be, the gem in the crown of this web site is the photo gallery. George has compiled one of the most extensive collection of automotive images on the net. There are literally thousands of images available ranging in topic from car culture to street rods.

348
Jimmy's Rods & Racing
http://www.gnat.net/~doodle

Jimmy's nice looking site is a tribute to Jimmy's past and present vehicles and NASCAR racing. There are numerous pictures of hot rods, Chevy trucks and more. Jimmy includes a '55 Chevy Truck page that gives information about Jimmy's '55 and photographs of it. There is a links page and a page with numerous photographs of hot rods and street rods.

Another page that Jimmy offers is the racing page, which is dedicated to Winston Cup in general and Jeff Gordon and Dale Earnhardt in particular. There is a current points standing as well as a Winston Cup schedule.

There is another page with VIN decoding information for '55–'59 Chevrolet trucks, and Jimmy offers his help in decoding other vintage truck numbers.

349
MJ's Roadster Web Page

http://www.algonet.se/~mj_t27/index.htm

Mikael Johansson, a rodder from Sweden, is notable because Mikael is the founder of one of the first web rings around. This popular web ring is known as the Street Rod Web Ring (SRWR).

On his site, Mikael offers a bit of information about his '27 Ford Roadster. There is also SRWR news, which details changes that take place on the SRWR. You can also apply to join the web ring and read the rules of the ring. The ring offered over 65 member sites when I visited the page. Mikael also maintains a guestbook.

350
Paul's Garage

http://members.tripod.com/~trucks/index1.html

Paul's Garage includes numerous interesting things for those looking to get an inside peek at the internal combustion engine. In addition to an overview of the internal combustion engine, there are sections on engine parts and how they work, currently including valve train, pistons and crankshaft. There is also advice on troubleshooting, car care, and how to do an overhaul on your motor starting with pulling the engine. There is even a section on cleaning. Visitors can also take a short "carparts" quiz.

There are personal links and car links, a small list of web rings, a guestbook and a Fix It Yourself Club, a Yahoo! Club founded by Paul, the owner of this site. There are also links to the Green Ribbon Campaign, which is a pro-trucker campaign to increase awareness of the problems facing truck drivers.

351
Riad's Dream Cars Home Page

http://www.geocities.com/MotorCity/Speedway/4388/index.html

This is a page by Riad Hanna, a sports car enthusiast from Melbourne, Victoria, Australia, with a thing for the Toyota Supra, the Supra MK-IV Twin Turbo to be precise. Although the Supra is Riad's favorite, the site itself includes numerous sports and exotic cars from around the world. The site provides a list of cars, each with its own page and 12 photographs (Riad invites readers to ask for more, if they should want them).

One of the best parts of this site, other than the extensive collection of photographs, is the Table of Performance. Here, a large number of cars' performance specifications are listed. The tables come from several sources, so each table or car does not have all of the following information, but most have 0–60, 0–100, 0–150 and 0–200 mph times, maximum speed, quarter mile time, power, MSRP, torque and several other bits of data.

Riad also maintains a list of links to other car sites and has a large list of car themes, or desktop pictures, both as downloads and as links to other theme creators' FTP sites. The themes are for Windows machines but can be made to work on a Mac with a bit of know-how.

352
Studebaker Under Construction — Dave Lester

http://www.provalue.net/studes

Dave Lester's page details the (de)construction of a '54 Studebaker Commander with over 30 photographs and details of each stage of the project.

The site also includes a guestbook and a number of good links. One is to the official alt.cars.studebaker web site, which is on the same server and also operated by Lester, but is a different web site. It details the regular members of the groups complete with photographs of them and their cars.

All in all, Studebaker Under Construction is one of the best "personal" home pages I have ever come across. If you love Studebakers, this is one stop that you cannot miss. Although it may take a few minutes to load, the pictures alone are worth the wait. It has to be one of the largest collections of Studebaker photos on the net.

Additional Web Sites

353 Smokin Joe's Hot Rod Page
http://snake.srv.net/~jxc/cars.html

354 The Best Damn Garage on the Net
http://home.sprynet.com/sprynet/pman01/

355 Car Stars of Film and Television
http://www.javelinamx.com/carstars/index.htm

356 Hepcat's Edsel Page
http://www.uslink.net/~hepcats/edsel.html

357 Tony McLean's MoPar Experience Page!
http://www.storm.ca/~moparman

358 The Hot Rod Page
http://members.tripod.com/~HotRod_32/index.html

359 Cameron's Home Page for VOLVO Admirers
http://infoweb.magi.com/~cvolvo

360 Mark Tsai's Web Page: R/C Cars
http://www.lemmings.com/mark/rccars.htm

361 DriftKing's Japanese Performance Cars
http://www.geocities.com/MotorCity/Garage/6175

362 Bill Jackameit's Studebaker Page
http://onyx.pvcc.cc.va.us/~wjackame/studpg.html

363 Ron's Hot Wheels Homepage
http://pages.prodigy.com/hotwheels.highway

364 Datsun Z Car
http://www.mame.mu.oz.au/salman/zpage.html

365 Moma's Car Page
http://users.aol.com/bonaphone/moma.html

366 Bott's MG Midget Page
http://members.tripod.com/~RBott

367 Muscle Car Heaven
http://home.earthlink.net/~jepereira/

12
RACING

There are a huge number of racing related sites scattered around the World Wide Web. Some of these sites are very large and comprehensive while others are small personal pages dedicated to a specific racer, team or series. There are also a large number of tracks, teams and drivers on the site.

This chapter will cover a range of all of the above and many professional and grassroots organizations.

368
Autocross.com
http://www.autocross.com

If you need information on the grassroots sport of autocross, this should be one of your first stops. If the site itself does not have the information, it will have links to sites that do. There are links to the "FAQ of Autocross" by John Crooke and the "Novice Handbook" by Kate Hughes. Autocross.com offers a car and driver of the week and a club of the week, plus information about the various SCCA car classes and rule updates. There are course worker requirements and various related rules. In autocross, you have to work the track as well as race it. This helps to keep the costs down and keep even weekend racers in the running. There is also an autocross calendar, a who's who of Autocross, an autocross club directory and links.

369
Autorace.com
http://www.autorace.com

Autorace.com has a huge number of articles about Formula 1 in particular. There are current year events, team information, an "F1 101" for the beginner, links, rankings, standings, schedule, a review of the past year and history of Formula 1 racing.

There is a large message forum under "Say It." You can also vote on certain F1 topics such as best team, best driver, best race and various others.

370
Carroll Shelby
http://carrollshelby.com

The adage "Carroll Shelby is alive and well and living under the hood" is certainly verified by Shelby's very own web site where you can learn almost anything about the living legend, Carroll Shelby. Shelby is perhaps one of the most universal of the automotive industry as his name is stuck on everything from late model Dodge Daytonas to the Shelby Oldsmobile and Dodge Durango S.P. 360 that appeared in 1998 to the famous and much duplicated AC (Shelby) Cobra, the car which he made famous in the sixties by combining a lightweight British body with raw American horsepower via big block Ford engines. This site presents what is currently transpiring in the life of Carroll Shelby and offers insights into his cars, his life and his passion for both of them. Carroll Shelby also makes public appearances, and there is a schedule of events and appearances on this web site.

Shelby is still cranking out hot cars with his name on them, and you can find out about the latest here. The site is also the place to find out about

Carroll's foundation, The Carroll Shelby Children's Foundation. Shelby underwent a heart transplant, and that opened his eyes to the difficulties that children face when they are suffering from serious medical conditions. The foundation was created in October of 1991 and has since helped five children get the critical care and treatment they need to successfully combat their illness. The foundation was created to assist children with acute coronary or kidney problems who cannot otherwise afford the treatment. The secondary goal of the foundation is to help fund organizations that are researching these illnesses. The site has information on how you can help the foundation.

371
Drag Racing List Online
http://www.draglist.com

The Drag Racing List, owned by Bill Pratt, is a large web site dedicated to drag racing of all types from sportsman to professional. Bill offers Bill's Notes as a journal of sorts which talks about drag racing, events connected with the site and other items that might interest the reader.

Danny White, a major supporter and drag racing nut, also has an editorial page on this site. There are numerous articles about drag racing and related topics — all makes, all races, all kinds of things. Along with this, there is a detailed history of the site plus how the site came to be in the first place and contributions people have made over the years.

The focus of the site is its list of 32,000 racers in 24 drag racing classes. There is detailed information on the racers, the machines they use and the races they race, plus other notes of interest. There is also a "readers' rides" section as well as the opportunity to download the entire list by contacting the webmaster of the site. This is also a great place to find historic information.

The list and the site in general are searchable, and you can fill out an entry form to list your own quarter mile glory. Links are provided to other drag racing sites around the web. You can also sign the guestbook, take a peek at all the awards this site has won and purchase videos, T-shirts, books, CDs, photographs and other merchandise.

372
Formula1.com
http://www.formula1.com

Formula1.com is a site that offers complete coverage of F1 events held around the world. It offers numerous articles, news, pictures, results, headlines, schedules and team information.

A "Fun" section includes web cards, links, a screen saver, a "babe" vote, games, Fantasy F1, a news group and caption competition. There are also interactive track maps, circuit statistics, team and driver info and other useful data. Each map is accompanied by travel and local information where available, notes on who has won on what particular track and other track-related information.

373
goracing.com
http://www.goracing.com
http://www.racezone.com

Goracing.com is one of the giants of racing related web sites. This site offers a vast collection of racing coverage on most mainstream types of racing in the United States, including current racing news and developments within the racing industry. There is also a racing related opinion poll so you can voice your opinion on current racing issues.

There are bulletin boards, which are divided up into three major sections. The Bench Racing section offers general racing talk for racers and enthusiasts. There is Fan Talk, where fans can discuss anything related to their favorite teams, drivers and anything else racing related, and finally the Swap Shop forum. Swap Shop is the place to post racing related items that you have for sale as well as to post want ads.

One of the more interesting areas is goracing.com's game room. This is the place to download commercial racing game demos or participate in goracing.com's very own NASCAR trivia challenge, which posts questions relating to NASCAR racing, its teams and its drivers.

There is an extensive multimedia library, where you can take a peek at video highlights, visit the photo gallery, take a look at readers' photographs and listen to RealAudio interviews with drivers and others in the vast sport of auto racing, visit the newsstand, read monthly articles about racing and get information on racing publications.

Visitors can also get detailed information and articles on race teams and tracks. A small selection of high and low profile teams in all aspects of the sport are featured, and there is a race schedule that lists many types of racing, including CART, Formula 1, IHRA, IRL, NASCAR, NHRA, WoO, and HAT. In addition to all of this, visitors can also check out the TV schedule for all the races mentioned above and search the entire goracing.com site.

All in all, goracing.com is probably one of the top three comprehensive racing sites on the net.

374
Indianapolis 500
http://www.indy500.com

Arguably the most famous of IRL races takes place at the Indianapolis Motor Speedway and is the Indianapolis 500. This is the ultimate Indianapolis 500 web site available on the net today. It features tips on how to find what you're looking for on the site, information on the availability of tickets, and race gear for sale such as hats, jackets, caps and other products.

Readers can get live timing and scoring, read the latest Indy 500 news and articles, browse an extensive photo gallery, see the cars, "tour" the track, read about the pace cars and get a little history on past pace cars. You can get the facts about your favorite drivers, including bios and photos; read about the Parade of Champions; visit the Recordbook to get info on race winners in the AAA and USAC eras of the track; and read about top rookies, records, milestones, the current season and many other topics.

375
iRACE
http://www.irace.com

One of the interesting things about iRACE is the Java–based games it has. There are currently two, an Indy style game and an oval track. If you have a Java–enabled browser, they are worth trying out. You can also "race" against the clock and see if your time makes it onto the board, where it will be displayed for a week. What a sneaky (and fun) way to build a mailing list!

In addition, iRACE is the home of a pretty good news section covering NASCAR, Formula One, IRL, drag racing, open wheel, road racing and stock cars. Each type of race has its own section with news, reviews and reports on what's happening in the sport. There are also message boards dedicated to the various leagues. You can plan your trips to the track with iRACE's complete racing schedule, and if you hear the drivers or commentators say something you don't quite understand, there is a glossary of racing terms located at this site as well. This feature is a rare resource among major racing sites that assume you already know everything.

There is no lack of interactivity at iRACE. In addition to the games, you can take part in the "Power Polls" or shop at the site's store for diecast models, shirts, apparel and other merchandise. You can check out the message boards, get the e-mail newsletter sent right to your computer or post a classified ad. When you're finished with all of that, stop by the photo album to check out great shots of the cars in action. There are also numerous articles and features that change regularly.

376
NASCAR Online
http://www.nascar.com

It is difficult to summarize a site as large and complex as NASCAR Online, the official site of NASCAR. Space in fact does not permit a full description, but suffice it to say that there is everything a fan could possibly want to know about NASCAR here. There are scores of articles on the basics, the teams, the cars, the tracks and every other facet of the sport. Read articles from drivers, team members and others in the industry. The site offers current and archived news, schedules, video and audio clips and more. You can check out the results, teams, newsstands, fans, standings, tracks and a NASCAR store. Simply put, NASCAR Online is probably the best NASCAR site on the net.

377
The North American Motorsports Pages
http://www.na-motorsports.com

The North American Motorsports Pages are a large collection of information about motorsports in North America. It focuses mainly on grassroots types of racing such as rally and autocross. These sorts of motor competition are big business in Europe, but relatively obscure in North America.

You can search the entire site by keyword. The site offers a Journal, which is an online magazine that covers racing in general plus rally and autocross. Back issues are available.

There is a large directory of organizations related to motorsports. Each entry includes links to the sites, overviews of the organization and contact information where applicable. Some of the sections include road racing, stock cars, sprints, midgets, motorcycles, autocross, rally, time trials and driving schools, plus a few sections that were under development at the time of my visit. Also included is information on road racing, oval racing and motorcycle racing.

There is an autocross section that gives a good overview of autocross, a discussion board, how to get started and links to other resources on the net. There is similar information on time trials, hill climbs and rally. The rally section covers road rallies, links, time-speed-distance plus how to find rallies in your area.

Also included on this web site is a large listing of driving and racing schools as well as information on race tracks. Road, oval, drag and kart tracks are covered. There are resources such as articles, links and mailing lists. You can also browse the gallery of SCCA and WoO images, sign the guestbook, post messages to the discussion board, catch up on results of road, circle, drag, autocross, time trial, hillclimb and rally racing, and finally visit the chat room. In the end, you can check out the credits.

378
Race Search
http://www.racesearch.com

Race Search offers over 7,000 links and resources for race enthusiasts. The site, divided into a number of distinct sections, is easy to use on the whole. Every now and then, however, the navigation bar along the top and bottom of the pages will disappear, almost forcing you to go back to the previous page in order to jump to the next section.

The "What's New" section includes all of the current Race Search press releases. Race Search is involved with a number of automotive companies on the net including Crower and Fuel Safe.

The primary focus of the site is its directory of racing related web sites, including advertisers, driving schools, events, general links and many other categories. Appropriate listings are divided further by state. Each link includes contact, address information and a description.

A large section is devoted to a track search. The tracks are divided into separate listings for Canada and the United States and then further broken down by province or state and then city. A huge number of tracks are listed here.

There is a monthly profile of a manufacturer, a track and an association. The site also offers "blowout" specials on items from the Race Search catalog. The catalog offers items ranging from performance parts to apparel.

379
RaceLink Motorsports
http://www.racelink.com

RaceLink offers daily racing news, and the news is archived by month. RaceLink also includes a directory of over 1,000 links to both race and general automotive sites. Sample topics include IndyCar, Formula One, NASCAR, Road Rally, Drivers, Teams, Driving Schools, Sponsors, Newsgroups, Car Museums and Miscellaneous. RaceLink also has fantasy leagues and a complete "Race Day" schedule.

You can browse the art gallery and submit your own art. There is also a Java–based chat room and a message board with two sections, one for buying and selling race tickets and one for fan discussion with no advertisements allowed.

RaceLink also offers a search engine with which you can search the RaceLink web site or the entire Internet. There is also a contact page and a section about sponsoring RaceLink.

380
Road America
http://www.roadamerica.com

Road America is a large track located in Elkhart Lake, Wisconsin. Its web site is filled with information about the track and the races that take place there. Included are directions to the track, information on food and lodging in the Elkhart Lake area and the latest news and video of the track.

There is a schedule of events taking place at Road America, and you can purchase tickets online. Many independent clubs hold their events at Road America, and there is a list of these events as well as contacts, dates and phone numbers. You can also browse the media guide and the photo gallery as well as a detailed track map.

There is also a Road America Fan Page which includes a kids' club, souvenirs, race shop and mailing list. Links are also provided.

381
Speed Mall / Racer Mall
http://www.speedmall.com
http://www.racermall.com

The Speed Mall takes the form of an advanced virtual mall, complete with multiple levels and a floor plan. At the time of my review the mall was not yet operational, but the tours of what was to come looked promising.

The Speed Mall has four major sections, or levels. Level one is the Championship Plaza, which offers a chat room and motorsports merchandise such as posters, jewelry, toys and books.

The second level houses the Club Plaza, which will provide virtual shoppers with an online community that offers driver fan clubs, kids' and teen clubs and more. There will also be club merchandise for sale.

The third level of the virtual Speed Mall is the Performance Plaza, which will be the home of performance parts for real race cars.

The fourth and final level is the Corporate Level, which will maintain a multimedia "theater," an auction service, race tickets and security information as well as information on the mall's management. The Speed Mall is part of the goracing.com web site.

382
Speedworld Online
http://www.speedworld.net

Speedworld is a large web site dedicated to all of the major racing series. This is probably one of the most extensive racing sites on the entire Internet.

Speedworld Online offers such features as chat, classified ads, a huge range of articles, scanner frequencies, historical articles, live audio coverage, links, media contacts, a message forum, news, pictures, team and track information, trivia, a TV schedule and racing headlines. The site also offers the usual point standings, results, schedules and statistics.

Among the more unusual features of this site are the fan views. These are articles written by fans, reviewed by Speedworld and then published in this special page on the web site.

383
Sports Car Club of America (SCCA)
http://www.scca.org

The SCCA is the sanctioning body for many of the grassroots motorsports that take place in the United States. It is a non-profit organization with over 55,000 members in 109 regions that hold over 2,000 events each year. A grassroots racing program is one in which the average person, with a bit of training and preparation, can jump into his or her daily driver and compete in formal events and race series throughout the season. There are some big-bucks cars that run in these races, too, but the average member-racer could be your next door neighbor. Another interesting thing about grassroots events is that members also help out. You may be a driver one day, but the next you'll have to watch the cones on the autocross track. This is one of the many things that keeps this hobby affordable for everyone. If everyone helps out, it works more smoothly and cheaply than leaving all the work and organization to the sanctioning body.

The SCCA has basically two distinct areas, with a few shades of gray in between. In the "amateur" competition division are club racing, Solo races, Pro Solo, road rally and PRO Rally. Each is a bit different from the others, but all of them generally take the form of either an autocross or a rally event. Along with detailed information on each event, there are applications and forms online, as well as the competition regulations for each event. On the "professional" side of the coin are Trans-Am, United States Road Racing Championship, Motorola Cup, V.S. F2000, and ACRL. All of the professional racing series have their own web sites but still fall within the SCCA realm.

You can also get information on SpeedFreakz, the SCCA's special program for younger drivers, as well as general information on how to get started in this world of motorsports. Along with all of this is general information on the SCCA, the SCCA in the news, press releases, regional information, SCCA membership, a region locator and so forth.

384
Summit Racing
http://www.summitracing.com

Summit Racing is one of the premier motorsports supply catalogs in the United States. Its site offers an online version of the extensive catalog of performance parts for street and strip. The online catalog is every bit as extensive as the print version, and you can order online. You can also order a free copy of the print catalog.

Summit's web site offers much more than just a catalog. You can get coverage on events around the United States, as well as numerous articles on featured cars that were built using Summit's parts. Each car is detailed with an overview as well as the specifics of what was used to build the car.

Another section is the Tech Zone. In the tech zone, you can ask Professor Overdrive your technical questions and read the archived tech tips and articles. Professor Overdrive also appears in the print catalog, as well as the featured cars mentioned above.

Summit not only preaches racing, but also practices it. Summit regularly builds high-end street/strip hot rods and participates in major drag racing competitions such as NHRA and IHRA events with its Summit cars and trucks. There are also race links, race news covering NASCAR, NHRA and IHRA, and a manufacturers' midway where you can link to the home pages of the manufacturers of the products that Summit offers in its catalog.

Finally, there is Drag Race Central, where you can get up-to-the-minute news on NHRA and IHRA racing.

Additional Web Sites

385 McLaren Online Magazine
http://www.mclaren.co.uk

386 Race Central
http://www.racecentral.com

387 Racing Point of View
http://www.autoracing.org

388 National Fantasy Racing League
http://www.nfrl.com

389 The Stock Car Gallery
http://www.stockcargallery.net

390 FanLinks.Com
http://www.fanlinks.com

391 Racetek
http://www.racetek.com

392 10 Tenths Motorsport
http://www.ten-tenths.com

393 The Racer Archive
http://student-www.eng.hawaii.edu/carina/ra.home.page.html

394 Race Car Sales Site
http://www.race-cars.com

395 Racecar
http://www.racecar.co.uk

396 Pro Racing Series
http://www.pro-racing.com

397 Race Cars for Sale
http://www.racecarads.com

398 Auto Race Museum
http://www.autoracemuseum.com

399 Goodyear Racing
http://www.goodyear.com/about/racing

400 Jet Racing
http://www.jetracing.com

401 ChasinRacin
http://www.chasinracin.com

402 Truck, Race, Cycle & Rec. Marketplace
http://www.truckracecycle.com

403 Race Cakes
http://www.fanpans.com

404 Auto Sport South Porsche Race Site
http://www.autosportsouth.com

405 Pikes Peak International Hill Climb
http://www.ppihc.com

13 WEB DIRECTORIES & SEARCH ENGINES

The Internet features nine or ten search engines and directories dedicated to the automobile and related subjects such as motorcycles. All of the directories feature at least 3,000 automotive links and often contain other features such as car pricing information, articles, reviews and more.

Along with this, each of the major "portals" has a specialized section usually called an auto "channel." These channels, also listed in this chapter, vary widely in quality and completeness. None of them offers the total number of sorted and cataloged links as the specific directories, but many offer auxiliary services such as pricing information and partnerships with other sites that provide additional automotive information.

There are currently several major web sites in the automotive search engine and directory category. Some are quite specialized; others are general guides. When it comes right down to it, almost all of them offer about the same number of links and each has pros and cons. Chances are you'll want to bookmark two or three of your favorites and visit the others when needed.

406
All Things Automotive
http://www.autodirectory.com

This site is one of the oldest and probably best known auto directories on the net. It offers links to over 3,000 automotive web sites within a variety of categories including classics, classified, clubs, interactive, motorcycles, parts and service, sports and more. There are currently 15 main categories represented on this site.

The Side Roads section collects articles by various writers on automotive topics. There are also event listings, local guides, four featured sites at any given time (which earn a link on the All Things Automotive home page), a bookstore, automotive news, classified ads and other attractions. The entire site is searchable. Visitors can also get advertising information and a free listing for their automotive sites.

You can also check out the site's category guides, which are overviews with detailed information about specific sections. All Things Automotive also rates most sites, offers reviews of some of them and provides a key to give you a glimpse of what the site may hold for you. Like most other auto directories, this one offers "enhanced link" services to get your site noticed more easily.

407
Autoguide.net
http://www.autoguide.net

Autoguide.net has recently been revised and now includes a vast quantity of links. They claim to include over 4,500 links in their database. From clicking through their sections that estimate seems to be a little high, but I certainly could be wrong.

Autoguide.net is an impressive directory, none-the-less. They also include articles, a complete site map, the Top 50 links, archived articles, miscellaneous FAQs, net events, books for sale, and headline news. Some of the links are reviewed.

408
Automobilesites.com
http://www.automobilesites.com

This newly formed automotive directory was just getting started at press time. It did, however, look promising.

409
Car-Stuff
http://www.car-stuff.com

Car-Stuff is a little plainer than the other directories, meaning that it uses what is known as "generation 1" design, which makes the site simple but not overly appealing visually. It does, however, feature a large number of links spread out into various sections. Car-Stuff offers web site design services and has been in existence since 1996.

410
Carlounge
http://www.carlounge.com

Carlounge is a large directory service based in the U.K. that provides links of interest to people around the world. Carlounge features products, quizzes, vehicles, a marketplace, motorsports, news and bulletin boards. It also has information on finance, insurance, leasing, pricing and warranties. You often have to dig through a few layers to get at the information you want, but when you get there it's worth the extra trouble.

411
CARtimes Automotive Directory
http://cartimes.com

CARtimes was created as an alternative to the other directories in late 1997. It provides a simple design that allows the user to navigate quickly through the pages. This site includes approximately 3,500 web sites in its database, and all are searchable through a simple search engine. Additional features of this site include the *CARtimes (e)Zine*, which is a monthly e-mail newsletter covering the automotive industry and new and used car pricing information in association with AutoWorld/VIS and others. The directory is arranged under a number of broad headings such as aftermarket, car buying, mobilia, racing and classics, and each link in the directory has a brief description.

412
Deja News: Automotive
http://www.dejanews.com/categories/Recreation/Automotive/

Deja News is a bit different from your average portal. Instead of offering web sites, it lists news group articles. Here you can search, post, browse and reply to articles written on USENET, simply through your browser. The usual way to post or read a USENET newsgroup is to use a special newsreader, which you can get at any good software site, such as TuCows (http://www.tucows.com).

413
FindMail: Categories: Automobiles
http://www.findmail.com/lists/Recreation%20and%20Sports/Automotive

Find auto related mailing lists.

414
Mining Co.—Automobiles
http://automobiles.miningco.com/msub8.htm

The Mining Co. maintains this large web directory and car site. The Mining Co. offers several services on all of its "channels," including links, features (articles), bulletin boards, chats, and event listings. Each of the web sites in the directory has a brief description.

The Mining Co. could be considered a "comprehensive" site but is positioned mainly as a directory. The Mining Co. returns "Server Too Busy" errors more that other sites, but often these are very short-lived and can be remedied by reloading the page.

415
Nerd World
http://www.nerdworld.com/nw97.html

Nerd World maintains an impressive automotive section that is divided into various detailed areas such as accessories, clubs, parts, security, auto sports, insurance, books, government, motorsports, personal pages and much more. There are also numerous featured links.

416
Redline-Search.Com
http://redline-search.com

Red-Line is an extensive search engine that used to specialize exclusively in the automotive aftermarket, but has recently expanded to include other topics as well. This simple search engine has several categories such as manufacturers, motorsports, off-road, tools and equipment, services, import and export, and reference. Each site is listed as a brief description and then links to another page that has a slightly longer description; you then link to the site from there.

Redline-Search.Com's parent site is the Automotive Tool & Equipment Expo web site located at http://www.automotivetools.com. Anybody who has an automotive related site can add a link to the directory.

Redline-Search.Com also offers a few other services, such as web site design and page hosting. Web design seems to be a popular sideline for many web sites.

417
Roadsters
http://www.roadsters.com

Roadsters is a large, simple directory that claims over 4,000 links. In addition to the directory there is information on various topics such as land speed records. The site presents a number of categories including magazines, Cobras, Corvettes, Vipers, drag racing, racing, sports cars, model car kits and quite a few more. Each link shows the name of the site and a very brief description. The only drawback is that the directory isn't searchable. Each section contains a brief introduction. Pages seem a tad slow to load, but that may be attributable to a temporary poor connection. The site itself is essentially text dominated, and each section is divided into separate subsections, which makes browsing the site easier.

418
Top Ten Links
http://www.toptenlinks.com/autos.htm

While not really a search engine, Top Ten Links fits into the category of "directory" in some fashion. It offers over 600 top ten lists such as resources, import automakers, domestic automakers, racing, car buying and others of interest. Something to keep in mind is that these, like most other "top" lists, are rather subjective in nature. There are other "top ten" lists out there with a totally different lineup.

419
Yahoo!: Autos
http://autos.yahoo.com

Yahoo!, king of the portal heap, enjoys the benefits of a large automotive channel. The sections are organized by vehicle manufacturer and the site offers other resources as well.

Mainstream Web Directories and Search Engines

Author's note: It is recommended that you start with the URL given here, but if that does not lead you to the proper page because of the ever-changing nature of the major portals, you can go directly to the main URL and then click on the "autos" section from there.

420 Excite: Autos
http://www.excite.com:80/autos

421 Galaxy: Automotive
http://galaxy.tradewave.com/galaxy/Leisure-and-Recreation/Automotive.html

422 HotBot: Cars Channel
http://www.hotbot.com/cars

423 Infoseek: Autos
http://www.infoseek.com/Topic/Automotive?tid=1803

424 Looksmart: Autos
http://www.looksmart.com/e53930/r?lm&ize&

425 Lycos: Autos
http://www.lycos.com/autos

426 Magellan: Cars & Trucks
http://www.mckinley.com/magellan/Reviews/Hobbies/Cars_and_Trucks/index.magellan.html

427 Search.Com: Autos
http://www.search.com/Single/0,7,0-750587,0200.html

428 Webcrawler: Autos
http://www.webcrawler.com:80/Auto

14
WOMEN'S FOCUS

There is a significant push on the Internet to target key audiences. One way to target these desirable audiences is to offer specific content keyed to their interest. The automotive industry is no exception to this trend, and a number of automotive web sites that cater to a female audience have sprung up over the past couple of years. If anything, it is surprising that there are not more. Some of these sites consist of a few tidbits of content surrounded by amazing amounts of fluff, others are very serious about their mission.

429
American Woman Motorscene
http://www.americanwomanmag.com

Although the current framed design can prove a little troublesome on a smaller monitor and a slow connection, this site offers a wealth of info complementary to the print magazine of the same name. The site features road tests, reviews, travel and safety information, news, profiles of pioneering women, humor, chat, links, subscription information, workshops and tips on owning a vehicle. This site is one of the best. My biggest gripe is the design, but content is king and in this respect it excels.

430
Auto Guide from Women.com
http://www.women.com/index/cars.html

Part of the extensive Women.com web site, this site includes cost calculators and articles on leasing, financing, safety and other relevant topics. Beatrice's Web Guide at http://www.bguide.com/webguide/cars/top.html serves as the links area.

There are dozens of links that shoot you all over the Women.com web site. I get the feeling that this is a small part of the Women.com web site and is mostly a token attempt at automotive content to serve reader demand.

431
Car Buying for Women
http://www.carbuyingforwomen.com

Car Buying for Women offers many of the same services that the AutoWorld home site offers: current new and used vehicle prices, featured vehicles, free price quotes, negotiating tips, safety information, financing tips, warranties and consumer alerts. The site is sponsored by AutoWorld (http://www.autoworld.com/).

432
Drag Racing Association of Women (DRAW)
http://www.drawfasthelp.org

DRAW is a volunteer charity organization that seeks to "[offer] financial and emotional support to individuals involved in drag racing accidents." The DRAW web site includes a catalog, through which you can support DRAW by purchasing racing related apparel and other related automobilia. The site also features information about DRAW's unique program. This includes the Injured Racer DRAW Spotlight, which spotlights injured racers, news, membership benefits and info on *DRAWing Attention*, DRAW's newsletter.

433
Elle Buying Guide
http://www.ellemag.com/buying_guide

Put on by Hachette Filipacchi Magazines under the *Elle Magazine* web site, this car buying guide offers basic information on manufacturers and vehicles. It is interactive to the point that you can input a manufacturer, price range and vehicle type and get detailed information and specs on particular vehicles that match your choices.

Also included on this site are financing, car care, and safety tips and classified ads per the *Elle*/Autoweb site at http://www.elle.autoweb.com.

434
Thunder Valley Racing
http://www.thunval.com

"Creating Opportunities for Women Drivers in Professional Racing" is the motto of this site for both drivers and fans, and effectively communicates the site's backing of female drivers in all forms of auto racing.

Features include links, an image gallery, biographies of drivers, a special weekly chat session with drivers, discussion boards and more. One of the best resources this site has to offer is the links to drivers' sites. If you race, this is one stop you shouldn't miss.

Another feature is *Distant Thunder*, the e-mail newsletter of Thunder Valley Racing.

435
Under the Hood — Women at the Wheel
http://www.womenatthewheel.com
http://www.under-the-hood.com

From the author of *The Greaseless Guide to Car Care*, Mary Jackson, this site features a Q&A section, factoids, tips on auto repair and that is about it. The content of these various sections is a bit limited. Overall, the site is surprisingly thin on material and serves essentially as an advertisement for the two books, *The Greaseless Guide to Car Care* and *Car Smarts*, both by Mary Jackson.

436
Woman Motorist
http://www.womanmotorist.com

The most extensive and informative of the "woman focused" automotive web sites is also one of the best of all the automotive sites on the Internet. The amount of information located here is simply staggering, and a pretty significant portion of it is from a woman's point of view. The layout is appealing and easy to follow with a large directory of the site located on the left side of the page.

Features include in-depth car reviews; tips; articles on such topics as car buying, maintenance, safety, racing, autocross, car law, and motorcycles; event listings, industry insider news, chat and much more.

There is also a bit of information on the Tread Lightly! program, and the site includes travel information and reader mail. One notable feature is FEMMETECH, an excellent Q&A on common automotive problems that motorists encounter on an everyday basis.

437
Women's Auto Help Center
http://www.womenautohelp.com

More narrowly focused than Woman Motorist, the Women's Auto Help Center bills itself as "A Special Place for Women with Questions about Cars." The only hitch here is that you have to register in order to get at all of the information contained on the site, although much is available without registration. Registration can be a lengthy process and requires that you fill out several large forms.

One of the innovative things about this site is that the articles are downloadable. This is great for those who find their eyes strained by reading on the monitor. Visitors do not have to register to get at the articles, which are the main focus of this site.

Features include Health, Your Mate, Style, Kids and more. All of the features tie in to automobiles in some fashion.

Additional Web Sites

438 Women's Wire: Buying a Car
http://womenswire.com/cars

439 Sarah Kavanagh: F1 Driver
http://www.irsrace.demon.co.uk

440 Marybeth's Motorsports Marketing Web Site
http://mach1-racing.com

441 ASE Women's Corner
http://www.asecert.org/tips/women/index.html

15
NEWSGROUPS

USENET is one of the older services that the Internet has to offer. It is a massive forum that features about 32,000 groups, all of which may not be available to you as the typical service provider is not likely to carry all of them; most carry around 30,000. Each of these groups can contain up to six or seven thousand individual messages. There are approximately 120 auto related USENET newsgroups. They are primarily "alt" and "rec" groups. USENET uses a very rigid naming structure: An "alt" group is the catch-all and the "alt" designation stands for "alternative," meaning that anything goes; the "rec" designation stands for "recreation" and focuses mainly on hobbies and leisure.

After you take a look at all the groups available, you will notice several other prefixes such as "misc" or "uk." The "uk" designation means the same thing that it does on a URL, namely that the group is focused on Great Britain.

Before posting to your heart's content on these groups, you should stop by a site such as Deja News and read up on USENET etiquette, as it has its own special set of unwritten rules, much like the World Wide Web.

442
Deja News: Automotive
http://www.dejanews.com/categories/Recreation/Automotive/

Deja News is a web site that allows you to read and post to newsgroups with a browser based interface, much like viewing a normal web site. While both Netscape Navigator and Microsoft Internet Explorer are able to read newsgroups in the traditional way, Deja News has made USENET simple and easy to use.

The Groups

443 *alt.american.automobile.breakdown*
444 *alt.auto.mercedes*
445 *alt.auto.parts.wanted*
446 *alt.autos*
447 *alt.autos.antique*
448 *alt.autos.audi*
449 *alt.autos.bmw*
450 *alt.autos.camaro*
451 *alt.autos.camaro.firebird*
452 *alt.autos.chevelle*
453 *alt.autos.chevrolet.malibu*
454 *alt.autos.classic-trucks*
455 *alt.autos.corvette*
456 *alt.autos.dean-stark*
457 *alt.autos.dodge.trucks*
458 *alt.autos.dsm*
459 *alt.autos.ferrari*
460 *alt.autos.ford*
461 *alt.autos.ford.festiva*
462 *alt.autos.ford.flathead*
463 *alt.autos.4x4.chevy-trucks*
464 *alt.autos.german*
465 *alt.autos.gm*
466 *alt.autos.gm.monza-hspecial*
467 *alt.autos.grand-national*
468 *alt.autos.grand.national*
469 *alt.autos.isuzu*
470 *alt.autos.italian*
471 *alt.autos.karting*
472 *alt.autos.macho-trucks*
473 *alt.autos.mini*
474 *alt.autos.mitsubishi*
475 *alt.autos.nissan*
476 *alt.autos.nissan.maxima*
477 *alt.autos.nissan.z-car*
478 *alt.autos.peugeot.sucks*
479 *alt.autos.porsche*
480 *alt.autos.porsche.911*
481 *alt.autos.porsche.944*
482 *alt.autos.rod-n-custom*
483 *alt.autos.rotary*
484 *alt.autos.saab*
485 *alt.autos.sport.nhra*
486 *alt.autos.sport.rally*
487 *alt.autos.studebaker*
488 *alt.autos.subaru*

489 *alt.autos.volvo*
490 *alt.binaries.models.scale*
491 *alt.binaries.pictures.autos*
492 *alt.binaries.pictures. drag-racing*
493 *alt.binaries.pictures.vehicles*
494 *alt.business.import-export. vehicles*
495 *alt.cars*
496 *alt.cars.ferrari*
497 *alt.cars.Ford-Probe*
498 *alt.cars.ford-probe*
499 *alt.cars.lotus*
500 *alt.consumers.auto-service*
501 *alt.hi-po.mopars*
502 *alt.hobbies.slotcars*
503 *alt.honda*
504 *alt.hotrod*
505 *alt.sport.dragracing*
506 *alt.trucks.chevy*
507 *alt.trucks.ford*
508 *alt.volkswagen.beetle*
509 *aus.cars*
510 *austin.autos*
511 *ba.market.vehicles*
512 *ca.driving*
513 *clari.biz.industry.automotive*
514 *clari.biz.industry. automotive.releases*
515 *clari.sports.motor*
516 *dc.driving*
517 *de.rec.sport.motor*
518 *fj.rec.autos*
519 *fj.rec.autos.sports*
520 *fj.rec.autos.wagon*
521 *it.sport.formula1.moderato*
522 *misc.transport.road*
523 *rec.auto*
524 *rec.auto.tech*
525 *rec.autos*
526 *rec.autos.antique*
527 *rec.autos.driving*
528 *rec.autos.4x4*
529 *rec.autos.makers.chrysler*
530 *rec.autos.makers.ford. explorer*
531 *rec.autos.makers.ford. mustang*
532 *rec.autos.makers.honda*
533 *rec.autos.makers.jeep+ willys*
534 *rec.autos.makers.mazda. miata*
535 *rec.autos.makers.saturn*
536 *rec.autos.makers.vw. aircooled*
537 *rec.autos.makers.vw. watercooled*
538 *rec.autos.marketplace*
539 *rec.autos.misc*
540 *rec.autos.rod-n-custom*
541 *rec.autos.simulators*
542 *rec.autos.sport*
543 *rec.autos.sport.f1*
544 *rec.autos.sport.indy*
545 *rec.autos.sport.info*
546 *rec.autos.sport.misc*
547 *rec.autos.sport.nascar*
548 *rec.autos.sport.rally*

549 *rec.autos.sport.tech*
550 *rec.autos.subaru*
551 *rec.autos.tech*
552 *rec.autos.vw*
553 *rec.toys.cars*
554 *relcom.wheels*
555 *tnn.rec.4wd*
556 *tnn.rec.motorsport*
557 *ukr.commerce.auto*
558 *uk.rec.motorsport.misc*
559 *uk.rec.cars.classic*
560 *uk.rec.cars.tvr*
561 *uk.rec.cars.vw.aircooled*
562 *wiz.bmw*
563 *wiz.mopar*
564 *wiz.motorace*
565 *wiz.roadsters*

16
MANUFACTURERS' SITES

Every major manufacturer has a web presence, and many of them even have web sites dedicated to specific models. Auto makers the world over have found the web a valuable no-pressure sales tool in which to showcase their automobiles and provide promotional materials such as press releases and brochures.

This chapter offers a simple listing of major and minor manufacturers from around the world. Manufacturers are always creating new sites in which to showcase specific automobiles, and there is no doubt that this list will continue to grow rapidly in the future.

566 Acura
http://www.acura.com

567 Alfa 156 Official Site
http://www.alfa156.com

568 Alfa Romeo
http://www.alfaromeo.com

569 Alfa Romeo Germany
http://www.alfaromeo.de

570 Alfa Romeo Netherlands
http://www.alfaromeo.nl

571 AM General Corporation
http://www.hummer.com/

572 Audi
http://www.audi.com/

573 Audi USA
http://www.audiusa.com/

574 BMW of Canada
http://www.bmw.ca/

575 BMW of North America
http://www.bmwusa.com/

576 Buick
http://www.buick.com/

577 Cadillac
http://www.cadillac.com/

578 Cadillac Europe
http://www.cadillaceurope.com/

579 Caterham
http://www.caterham.co.uk

580 Celco Profil
http://www.celcoprofil.com

581 Chevrolet
http://www.chevrolet.com

582 Chrysler
http://www.chryslercars.com/

583 Chrysler Corporation Technology Center
http://www.chryslercorp.com/

584 Chrysler Investor Relations Web Site
http://www.investor-rel.com/

585 Chrysler Media Relations Web Site
http://www.media.chrysler.com

586 Citroen
http://www.citroen.it

587 Citroen Suisse
http://www.citroen.ch

588 Daewoo Motor Company
http://www.dm.co.kr/

589 DAF Trucks
http://www.daftrucks.com

590 Daihatsu Netherlands
http://www.daihatsu.nl

591 Daimler-Benz
http://www.daimler-benz.com/

592 DaimlerChrysler
http://www1.daimlerchrysler.com/

593 Dodge
http://www.4adodge.com/

594 Duesenberg Motors, Inc.
http://www.duesenbergmotors.com/

595 Eagle
http://www.eaglecars.com/

596 Encore Vehicles
http://www.encorevehicles.com

597 Excellence Motor Carriages
http://www.i-magine.com/excellence/

598 Ferrari
http://www.ferrari.com

599 Ferrari Italy
http://www.ferrari.it/ferrari/

600 Fiat
http://www.fiat.com

601 Ford Motor Company
http://www.ford.com

602 Ford Motor Company Japan
http://www.ford.co.jp

603 Ford Motor Company Online Shopping Service
http://olss.ford.com

604 Ford Motor Company UK
http://www.ford.co.uk

605 Freightliner Corporation
http://www.freightliner.com

606 General Motors
http://www.gm.com

607 GMC
http://www.gmc.com/

608 Holden Special Vehicles
http://www.hsv.com.au/

609 Honda
http://www.honda.com/

610 Honda Australia
http://www.honda.com.au/

611 Hyundai Korea
http://www.hmc.co.kr/

612 Hyundai USA
http://www.hyundaiusa.com/

613 Infiniti G20
http://www.g20.com/

614 Infiniti Motors
http://www.infinitimotors.com

615 Isuzu
http://www.isuzu.com/

616 Italdesign
http://www.italdesign.com

617 Jaguar S-Type
http://www.jaguar-s-type.com

618 Jaguar USA
http://www.jaguarcars.com

619 Jeep Home Page
http://www.jeepunpaved.com

620 Kia of Germany
http://www.uni-x.net/Firmen/Kia/welcome.html

621 Kia of North America
http://kia.com/

622 Lamborghini
http://www.lamborghini.com

623 Lancia of Italy
http://com-e.iol.it/lancia/y/e/

624 Land Rover
http://www.landrover.com

625 Land Rover Freelander
http://www.freelander.de

626 Land Rover North America
http://www.best4x4.landrover.com

627 Land Rover South Africa
http://www.landrover.co.za/

628 Land Rover Switzerland
http://www.landrover.ch/

629 Lexus
http://www.lexus.com

630 Lexus of Australia
http://www.lexus.com.au

631 Lexus USA
http://www.lexususa.com/

632 Lincoln
http://www.lincolnvehicles.com/

633 Lotus
http://www.lotuscars.com/

634 Mazda Canada
http://www.mazda.ca

635 Mazda UK
http://www.mazada.co.uk

636 Mazda USA
http://www.mazadausa.com

637 Mercedes-Benz
http://www.mercedes-benz.com/

638 Mercedes-Benz ML320
http://www.mbusa.com/models/ml320.html

639 Mercedes-Benz USA
http://www.usa.mercedes-benz.com/

640 Mercury
http://www.mercuryvehicles.com/

641 Mitsubishi Motors Japan
http://www.mitsubishi-motors.co.jp/

642 Mitsubishi Motors USA
http://www.mitsucars.com/

643 Morgan Motor Company
http://www.morgan-motor.co.uk

644 Mosler Automotive
http://www.moslerauto.com

645 Nissan Japan
http://www.nissan.co.jp/

646 Nissan USA
http://www.nissanmotors.com/

647 Oldsmobile
http://www.oldsmobile.com/

648 Oldsmobile Intrigue
http://www.intriguecar.com/

649 Opel
http://www.opel.com/

650 Opel Japan
http://www.opel.co.jp/

651 PACCAR Corporate Home Page
http://www.peterbilt.com

652 Panoz Auto Development Company
http://www.panozauto.com

653 Passat
http://www.passat.de/

654 Peugeot
http://www.peugeot.com/

655 Peugeot UK
http://www.peugeot.co.uk/

656 Plymouth
http://www.plymouthcars.com/

657 Pontiac
http://www.pontiac.com

658 Porsche
http://www.porsche.com

659 Porsche Belgium
http://www.porsche.be/

660 Porsche Motorsport North America
http://www.porschemotorsports.com/

661 Proton
http://www.proton.co.uk

662 PT Astra International
http://www.astra.co.id

663 Renault Belgique
http://www.renault.be

664 Rolls-Royce and Bentley Motor Cars
http://www.rolls-royceandbentley.com

665 Rover
http://www.rover.co.uk

666 Rover Group
http://www.rovergroup.com

667 Rover Group Haendlerverband Deutschland E.V.
http://www.rovernet.de

668 Rover Netherlands
http://www.rover.nl

669 Saab
http://www.saabusa.com/

670 Saab Automobile AB
http://www.saab.com

671 Saturn
http://www.saturncars.com/

672 Seat France
http://www.seat-france.com

673 Seat Germany
http://www.seat.de

674 Seat International
http://www.seat-international.com

675 Shelby American, Inc.
http://www.shelbyamerican.com/

676 Skoda
http://www.skoda auto.cz

677 Skoda France
http://www.skoda-france.com

678 Solectria Corporation
http://www.solectria.com/

679 Ssangyong Motors
http://symc.ssy.co.kr/english/e_index.htm

680 Subaru
http://www.subaru.com/

681 Subaru (Finland Suomi)
http://www.im-suomi.com/im-suomi

682 Subaru of Canada
http://www.subaru.ca/

683 Subaru of Cyprus
http://www.subaru.cy.net/

684 Subaru of Germany
http://www.subaru.de/

685 Subaru of Hong Kong
http://www.subaru.com.hk/

686 Subaru of Moscow
http://www.subaru.ru/

687 Subaru of Turkey
http://www.subarutr.com/

688 Suzuki
http://www.suzuki.be/

689 Tatra Czech Republic
http://www.tatra.cz

690 Tornado Sports Cars
http://www.tornado-ts40.com

691 Toyota
http://www.toyota.be/

692 Toyota Australia
http://www.toyota.com.au/

693 Toyota Japan
http://www.toyota.co.jp/

694 Toyota USA
http://www.toyota.com/

695 TVR
http://www.tvr-eng.co.uk

696 Yulon Motor Company, Ltd.
http://www.yulon-motor.com.tw

697 Vauxhall
http://www.vauxhall.co.uk/

698 Vaz Russia
http://www.vaz.ru

699 Volkswagen Australia
http://www.volkswagen.com.au

700 Volkswagen Brazil
http://www.volkswagen.com.br/

701 Volkswagen Germany
http://www.vw-online.de/

702 Volkswagen of America, Inc.
http://www.vw.com/

703 Volvo of North America
http://www.volvocars.com/

704 Volvo of Sweden
http://www.volvo.se/

705 Volvo UK
http://www.volvocars.volvo.co.uk

17
OTHER WEB SITES

This chapter provides a catch-all of web sites that are worth the mention but don't fit any other category.

706 AUTOdealerjobs.com
http://www.autodealerjobs.com

707 AUTOSHOP-Online!
http://www.autoshop-online.com

708 Chevy Mania!
http://www.chevymania.com

709 Hennessey Motorsports
http://www.hennesseyms.com

How do you make a Dodge Viper go even faster? Or make your Prowler, Durango or Ram V10 into a serious performance machine? Send it to John Hennessey and Hennessey Motorsports in Houston, Texas, U.S.A.

710 Import Performance Page
http://www.lycaeum.com

711 Locator On-Line — Automotive Recycling
http://www.partslocator.com

712 Rovers North
http://www.roversnorth.com

713 Truckworld Online
http://www.truckworld.com

714 *West of Laramie*
http://www.comm.wayne.edu/staff/wright/autohistory/00.html

West of Laramie is an online book written by Richard A. Wright, an assistant professor of journalism in Wayne State University's Communication Department of the College of Fine, Performing and Communication Arts (which must be hard to fit on a business card).

Like any book, it is divided into chapters, 23 of them to be exact, and is accompanied by "The Automobile in History: A Photo Portfolio" by Jenny King. The photo portfolio contains 100 years of automotive history in 28 sections and includes different types of cars ranging in style from funeral cars to trucks, muscle cars, woodies, phaetons and others.

Index

References are to entry numbers